SUCCESSFUL
TEAM BUILDING

The WorkSmart Series

The Basics of Business Writing
Commonsense Time Management
How to Speak and Listen Effectively
Successful Team Building

SUCCESSFUL TEAM BUILDING

THOMAS L. QUICK

amacom

AMERICAN MANAGEMENT ASSOCIATION
THE WORKSMART SERIES

Library of Congress Cataloging-in-Publication Data

Quick, Thomas L.
    Successful team building / Thomas L. Quick.
        p.   cm.—(The WorkSmart series)
    ISBN 0-8144-7794-1
    1. Work groups. I. Title. II. Title: Team building.
III. Series.
HD66.Q53   1992
658.4'02—dc20   92-3224
                                                   CIP

Printing number

20   19   18   17   16

CONTENTS

114076

PREFACE

The team concept has traditionally been very important in most organizations. You frequently hear the expressions "teamwork" and "being a team player." Yet despite the widespread talk about team effort, it's probably true that most people, on the work scene or in their personal affiliations, have not actually had a true team experience. People can work in the same department for years, serve on committees, meet in management groups regularly, and still not be a part of a team.

To function effectively, members of a team must be flexible, trusting of the other team members, and wholeheartedly supportive of every member of the group in its progress toward its goals. Perhaps one of the best examples of true teamwork is that of the surgical team, which is headed usually by a surgeon and includes surgical assistants, nurses, the anesthetist, and technicians. Each function is specialized and highly skilled, and each person knows that his or her success is dependent on the other members of the team. All are committed to the one objective: the well-being of the patient. Like most teams, the operating room group has taken a substantial amount of time to develop its effectiveness.

Team building helps a group function as a unit—it fosters morale, trust, cohesiveness, communication, and productivity. This book discusses that process from the point of view of the team leader. Here you'll learn how to:

- Build team commitment.
- Deal with team conflict.
- Use creativity in team problem solving and decision making.
- Use evaluation and rewards to determine team growth and reinforce its effectiveness.

T.Q.

PART

THE NATURE
AND BENEFITS
OF A TEAM

CHAPTER 1

WHAT IS A TEAM?

The most distinguishing characteristic of a team is that its members have, as their highest priority, the accomplishment of team goals. They may be strong personalities, possess highly developed specialized skills, and commit themselves to a variety of personal objectives they hope to achieve through their activity; but, to them, the most important business at hand is the success of the group in reaching the goal that its members, collectively and with one voice, have set. The members support one another, collaborate freely, and communicate openly and clearly with one another.

Most nonteam groups, on the other hand, tend to be collections of personalities with their own agendas, which may be more valuable to those personalities than the agenda that the majority of the group members seek to fulfill. Discussions and relationships in such groups are often characterized by shifting agendas, power subgroups, a going along with decisions rather than a wholehearted commitment, and even a win-lose orientation: One person or subgroup gains its wishes over another.

Don't let your vision get diluted, but don't be afraid of teamwork.

—JAMES B. PATTERSON CHAIRMAN, J. WALTER THOMPSON NORTH AMERICA

KINDS OF TEAMS

There are many kinds of groups that can evolve into closely knit teams. Some of the most common are:

- *Committees,* which usually serve as investigative or advisory bodies reporting to the person or agency that has appointed and organized them.
- *Task forces,* which, most often, are temporary problem-solving groups formed to deal with issues that cross

Characteristics of Effective and Ineffective Teams

Effective	Ineffective
Information	
Flows freely up, down, sideways	Flows mainly down, weak horizontally
Full sharing	Hoarded, withheld
Open and honest	Used to build power
	Incomplete, mixed messages
People relationships	
Trusting	Suspicious and partisan
Respectful	Pragmatic, based on need or liking
Collaborative	
Supportive	Competitive
	Withholding
Conflict	
Regarded as natural, even helpful	Frowned on and avoided
	Destructive
On issues, not persons	Involves personal traits and motives
Atmosphere	
Open	Compartmentalized
Nonthreatening	Intimidating
Noncompetitive	Guarded
Participative	Fragmented, closed groups
Decisions	
By consensus	By majority vote or forcing
Efficient use of resources	Emphasis on power
Full commitment	Confusion and dissonance
Creativity	
More options	Controlled by power subgroups
Solution-oriented	
	Emphasis on activity and inputs
Power base	
Shared by all	Hoarded
On competence	On politicking, alliances
Contribution to team	Pragmatic sharing
	Contribution to power source
Motivation	
Commitment to goals set by team	Going along with imposed goals
Belonging needs satisfied	Coercion and pressure

| More chance for achievement through group | Personal goals ignored Individual achievement valued without concern for the group |

Rewards

| Based on contribution to group Peer recognition | Basis for rewards unclear Based on subjective, often arbitrary appraisals |

functions or lines of authority. A task force may, for its life, be full- or part-time.

- *Quality circles,* consisting of groups of employees and supervisors who search for ways to increase the effectiveness of their work groups through higher productivity and improved quality.
- *Project groups,* organized to work specifically on a project, such as a new product, a new facility, or a computer program. Like the task force, the project group may have a temporary existence. When its mission has been accomplished, the group disbands.

Probably the most ambitious and complex team-building effort involves an entire work section or department, if only because in an ongoing operation the objectives change, requiring periodic review and goal-setting sessions among those who must commit and recommit themselves.

DIAGNOSING YOUR GROUP

A logical place to start your team-building effort is to look carefully at the group you manage or participate in. How is the group characterized? Complete the following diagnosticator. How many of the statements are true about your team?

(Text continues on page 9.)

GROUP DIAGNOSTICATOR

Consider each statement in terms of whether it characterizes your group or not. If the description is relevant rarely, treat the statement as if it does not apply. If it does, indicate with a check whether you observe it frequently or just occasionally.

	Fre-quently	Occa-sionally	Rarely/Never
1. Members of the group seek me out to talk about what they see going on in the group, or to complain about the lack of progress or cooperation.	☐	☐	☐
2. There are complaints that we spend too much time in meetings.	☐	☐	☐
3. Some members seem to feel that they do not get the information they need in a timely manner.	☐	☐	☐
4. Group decisions that I think have been made and agreed to have to be reopened and revised.	☐	☐	☐
5. People bring suggestions for improving the group's effectiveness to me.	☐	☐	☐
6. When new ideas are introduced, there seems to be more interest in what is wrong with them than in how they might work.	☐	☐	☐
7. In meetings, I get frustrated over interminable discussions that don't end up anywhere.	☐	☐	☐

	Fre-quently	Occa-sionally	Rarely/Never
8. Some members have more information than others about developments in the department and in the organization.	☐	☐	☐
9. There are some strong egos in the group, and this makes it hard for everyone to participate fully.	☐	☐	☐
10. Someone has to intervene in group discussions to keep them focused on the objective.	☐	☐	☐
11. Decisions of the group are really compromises.	☐	☐	☐
12. Members of the group have a confrontational style.	☐	☐	☐
13. Agreement and harmony characterize our group discussions.	☐	☐	☐
14. Decisions are arrived at by majority vote.	☐	☐	☐
15. I don't get feedback from others in the group about my leadership.	☐	☐	☐
16. People don't listen to one another.	☐	☐	☐
17. Some people try to take over group discussions and act on their personal agendas.	☐	☐	☐
18. Politicking goes on quietly and behind the scenes.	☐	☐	☐
19. People ask, "What are we trying to do? What's the point of all this?"	☐	☐	☐

(continues)

Group Diagnosticator (continued)

	Fre-quently	Occa-sionally	Rarely/Never
20. People cooperate with one another only when I show them it is important to do so.	☐	☐	☐
21. There are some people who lead, and they can be expected to take control early in the group discussion.	☐	☐	☐
22. Our group discussions keep covering the same ground.	☐	☐	☐
23. People get defensive when they meet resistance to their ideas.	☐	☐	☐
24. Partisan subgroups form around major issues.	☐	☐	☐
25. I ask people to leave personalities out of our discussions.	☐	☐	☐
26. Some people withdraw from participating in discussions.	☐	☐	☐
27. Disagreement degenerates into wrangling and nit-picking.	☐	☐	☐
28. Some people seem to value scoring points above everything else.	☐	☐	☐
29. I hear people say, "What's the use of speaking up?"	☐	☐	☐
30. Various members ask me to take sides.	☐	☐	☐

Subtotals	———— ×1	———— ×2	———— ×3	
Total Scores	————	+ ————	+ ————	
Grand Total			= ————	

For each "frequently" that you checked, give yourself a score of 1. "Occasionally" merits 2, and "rarely/never" rates 3. Multiply each number by the total number of statements to which you applied it. To illustrate, if you checked "occasionally" 10 times, "frequently" 10 times, and "rarely/never" 10 times, your overall score would be 60.

ANALYZING YOUR DIAGNOSIS

The higher your score, the more advanced your group in building itself toward team status. If your score is the maximum of 90 (30 times 3), you can count yourself exceptional indeed—and fortunate to have such an effectively functioning group without any (or nearly any) indicators of impediments or barriers to successful team operation. Conversely, if your score is 30, by no means can you describe your group as a team. If your total falls between 60 and 90, you are well on your way, but you still have some distance to travel before you and your associates can enjoy the plentiful benefits of working as a team rather than as a mere group.

Here are some of the meanings behind each statement:

1. If other members of the group talk to you about what is or is not going on in the group, that means a great deal of communicating occurs outside the group. The group's progress or lack of it, to members, is not a group issue, to be discussed in and dealt with by the group as a whole. Group issues in a team are handled by the team as a team, not by members of it in outside conferences.

2. The group has not yet learned how to conduct effective meetings in which, because of good formal and informal leadership, the group focuses on its goals and the best ways to achieve them. In a successful meeting, members support one another in working toward goals, ward off any attempts to sidetrack the discussion, and progress toward objectives.

3. A healthy team makes sure that all information necessary for its effective function is available to all members. The information moves up, down, and sideways. It is an open system, with inputs, throughputs, and outputs.

4. When decisions have to be remade, it is often because they were not made initially by consensus; the team did not take sufficient time to ensure that all members contributed fully and freely. There may also be a problem with the lack of completeness of needed information at the time of the decision; thus, the issue has to be reopened when the additional information is available.

5. Again, this extragroup activity prevents the group from coalescing and working together on what are properly group issues.

6. The group members are not acting as a team in which there is support for anything that might advance the team toward its goals. Too many personal agendas create competition, so ideas are shot down when they threaten anyone. And the group is not taking action as a team to make sure that the contributors are supported and their ideas are given sufficient consideration.

7. In an effective team, everyone in the group takes some responsibility for making sure that the group stays on track in its discussions. When the discussions are interminable, it means that no one is minding the store.

8. The information is not being disseminated. Some people are finding things out and are perhaps withholding the data from others in the group. It could mean a power play on the part of those who know, or it could simply be that no one is assuming the responsibility for seeing that the information gets around. People are acting for themselves rather than for the team.

9. When some members seem to dominate, others must assert themselves and act as gatekeepers for all members of the group. (See Chapter 7.)

10. Probably too many personal agendas are operating and competing with one another. There is insufficient concern for achieving team goals.

11. Compromises usually mean that everyone has to give up something, which means no one ends up really happy. The group should take longer to arrive at consensus, where everyone is convinced that the best decision possible has been made.

12. The term *confrontational style* often means that people are attacking other people rather than the issues, in which case conflict and resentment impede the progress of the group in doing its proper work. When people in a team confront only issues, the work gets done. But it takes training to help members differentiate between people and issues.

13. It's doubtful that a team doing serious work will appear in agreement and harmony all the time. Chances are that this group is backing off from anything that brings out conflict, anger, and disagreement, and such avoidance isn't characteristic of a true team.

14. The minority team members may feel that they have lost. Consensus decisions are better in that everyone wins.

15. Members of the group are withholding feedback that you need in order to be effective. Are they intimidated by you? Do they not trust you? Have you inadvertently discouraged feedback from them in the past? If a deficiency in communicating exists, you need to find out why.

16. Too many personal agendas are operating. The group is fragmented. The members do not listen to or support one another because they are not yet committed to group goals.

17. The answer for 16 applies here.

18. When people in a team seek support, they do so openly and in the group. Extragroup activity is destructive in team building.

19. The discussions apparently ramble and are unfocused. Where is the formal and informal leadership that helps clarify the issues and keeps the group on track?

20. People in a true team not only cooperate but collaborate. That is, they don't go along because someone convinces them they should do so. They willingly invest themselves in the group project. They want to be a part of the solution or result. That's collaboration.

21. The people who regularly step in to take control see a vacuum, and they move to fill it. Others sit back passively and permit them to do it. Leadership in a true team is passed from member to member. Everyone in a healthy group becomes a leader at some time or other.

22. It is possible that no one is assuming sufficient leadership to make sure the group's needs and goals are met. This statement describes a bunch of people sitting around and talking rather aimlessly.

23. Defensiveness may occur when people feel attacked or see no support within the group for their contributions. When a group is supportive and gives encouragement to its members, there is less defensiveness. When defensiveness does occur, group members move swiftly to perform certain roles that reduce the contributor's sense of isolation or attack. (See Chapter 7.)

24. These people are still wedded to their agendas and to taking control rather than to advancing the interests of the group as a whole.

25. If you have to ask people regularly to leave personalities out, then the group is dysfunctional, if only in the fact that other members of the group should insist on issues-based discussion as well as you.

26. When people withdraw from discussions, it often means that they feel no one really cares whether they participate or not. A team would move quickly to reassure them, to invite them to rejoin the discussion, and to make them feel valued. Another reason for withdrawal is that the person feels attacked and the withdrawal is protective. Once again, the group should provide support.

27. When people disagree—and that's normal in a vibrant, healthy group—other members can help to resolve conflicts, to find common ground, and to make the disagreement between two or more an issue for the whole group so that it becomes diffused.

28. Personal agendas and interpersonal competition destroy groups.

29. They believe that no one listens to them, supports their right to participate, or cares what they have to offer.

30. This refers to the "politicking outside" issue, which, as has been mentioned, can be deadly to the growth of the group.

CHAPTER 2

THE BENEFITS OF A TEAM

Working in teams results in benefits for both team members and the organizations in which they work. *Collaboration* is the primary benefit. People want to work well together, to support one another, because they identify with the team. They want the team to shine and be successful. Individual competitiveness is reduced. For the sake of the group, people want to do more than cooperate with one another. They collaborate; they willingly invest themselves in the team effort.

People who have learned to support and trust one another share what they know freely. They realize how important it is to the team to pass on the information that members need to operate more effectively. Information flows freely up and down and sideways. And so *communication* is another benefit. There is also a more efficient application of *resources*, talents, and strengths, because people are applying them willingly and sharing them with other members of the team. Whenever one member of a team lacks certain knowledge or competence, another is there to fill the gap.

A fourth benefit is *decisions and solutions*—made simultaneously, with everyone generating and evaluating more options than one person can develop. Lead time for implementation is reduced because people make their choices together and not sequentially, as often happens. Decisions are by consensus, which means they are usually better than what even the brightest person in the work group could come up with alone.

People who are responsible for decisions and solutions own them, and consequentially they feel *committed* to carrying them out successfully—the fifth benefit. Team members also feel a strong commitment to the team itself, not to let it down.

> **Once we've figured this out, we won't have this problem again—if we can remember how we did it.**
>
> **—WARD RINEHART JOHNS HOPKINS UNIVERSITY**

13

And last is *quality*. There is a concern for achieving quality and accuracy, because employees feel they are part of a team effort and want to make the team look as good as possible. In addition, because team members work collaboratively, they are ensuring that each member gets what he or she needs from the team to turn out the best possible work.

CHAPTER 3

LEADERSHIP IN
TEAM BUILDING

If you wish to build an effective team in your department, you must demonstrate a style of managing that contributes to greater participation by your subordinates in decision making and implementation. How acceptable to you is the idea of sharing your leadership? To answer this question, complete the following self-assessment. It will point out areas in which you can achieve more subordinate participation by altering your style.

ANALYZING YOUR DIAGNOSIS

These statements describe a participative management style, in which leadership is shared by subordinates and their manager. The more statements you checked as reflecting your own prevailing (as opposed to occasional) style, the greater the contribution you can make to the building of an effective team in your department.

STEPS TOWARD IMPROVEMENT

This self-assessment may suggest certain steps you can take to create a more participative environment for your employees or people you supervise. This is the time for you to think specifically about those steps.

Decision Making

Following are some thought starters to help you develop an action plan for yourself in important functional areas.

LEADERSHIP SELF-ASSESSMENT

Check off those statements that fairly reflect your present prevailing management style. If the statement does not reflect your style, simply leave the box blank.

1. I regularly involve employees in decision-making on issues that affect them and their ability to perform well on the job. ☐

2. I make sure that there is a steady flow of information both up and down. ☐

3. I treat my subordinates as partners and resources. ☐

4. In meetings, I encourage all present to participate in a full discussion and then arrive at consensus decisions. ☐

5. When we solve problems in the department, I encourage employees to seek a better alternative to whatever situation exists now. I discourage attempts to assign blame or responsibility for the problem. ☐

6. When subordinates give me feedback about my managing and operation, I let them know how much I appreciate their openness even though I may be distressed by what they tell me. ☐

7. I regard conflict and disagreement as inevitable in a vibrant, dynamic work group. ☐

8. I reward those employees who look for ways to increase their effectiveness and that of others. ☐

9. I do not feel less of a manager when I delegate any of my authority and responsibilities, share decision making with subordinates, or permit them to develop their own methods for accomplishing their tasks so long as those methods meet my performance standards. ☐

10. I believe that employees will commit themselves to the achievement of my goals and those of the department so long as they see an opportunity to accomplish their personal goals and to achieve satisfaction in doing so. ☐

11. I share what information I have about the organization, its policies, and its plans with subordinates, except for whatever higher management labels confidential. ☐

12. Most people at work, I believe, are motivated by the desire to grow in their skills and competence. ☐

13. When I see examples of collaboration between employees, I find some way to show my recognition of it and appreciation for it. ☐

14. When I must get employee acceptance of new policies and rules that come down from higher management, I use persuasion and influencing skills. ☐

15. In my department, employees know that they will be rewarded for good performance. ☐

16. I believe that the more people are involved in setting objectives, the more committed they usually are to achieving them. ☐

17. Even when I must impose certain changes because they have been set by higher management, I make sure that employees understand the rationale behind them, and even though I cannot alter the changes, I listen carefully to my subordinates' reaction to them. ☐

18. My people, I believe, look at increased responsibility as both a reward for good past performance and a means to grow and advance. ☐

19. I make sure that my criticism of a subordinate's performance is seen as evidence of my desire to help that person be more effective and get more of the results that both of us want. ☐

20. I am consistent in using both monetary and nonmonetary rewards to recognize those employees who have reached my goals and observed my work standards. ☐

21. I present performance evaluations as a means for employees to improve their effectiveness. ☐

Bringing the Group Together

How can you bring these affected employees and resources together to make a group decision? By consensus? When? How will you phrase the issue so as not to eliminate some worthwhile options? For example, if you were experiencing intense price competition on the West Coast, you would wish to avoid unnecessarily restrictive questions, such as "How can we get our goods to the West Coast and keep costs competitive?" The option you're excluding would be to produce the goods on the West Coast. Instead, you might phrase the question this way: "How can we sell competitively and profitably on the West Coast?" You may find that, in fact, you cannot.

Communicating

Do you have information about the organization that would be interesting to your people and that you have not transmitted? Are there areas and functions in your department of which your knowledge is not complete or up-to-date? Are there organizational changes forthcoming that your people need to know about? If so, how will you explain those changes? How

- What important issues are before you that press for attention or resolution?

  _____

  _____

  _____

  _____

- Which of your subordinates would those decisions affect?

  _____

  _____

  _____

  _____

- Which of your subordinates, while not directly involved in the issue or affected by the decision, nonetheless have experience, knowledge, or other resources that would contribute to an effective decision?

  _____

  _____

  _____

  _____

can you persuade your employees that they should accept such changes—or that they might even benefit from them? Do you welcome feedback from your employees, listen actively to it, let them know that you have heard it, and then thank them for having brought feedback to you? Is there an employee whom you must criticize for a performance deficiency? If so, how can you frame your criticism so as to convince him or her that you want to help in increasing effectiveness?

Goal Setting

Do you periodically and regularly sit down with your employees and explain what you expect from them in accomplishing

- Take one of the issues that you'd like a group decision on and write it down, being careful not to eliminate any options unnecessarily.

  _____

  _____

  _____

  _____

- What restrictions—for example, money, personnel, time—do your team members need to know about before they develop and explore options?

  _____

  _____

  _____

  _____

- Using the action plan model just described, examine some of the other steps you can take, listing the people involved (either because they are affected or because they are resources), the issues, action steps, and so forth.

  _____

  _____

  _____

  _____

your goals? Do you invite them, where possible, to help you set goals? Do you make sure that you get feedback from them on whether they view your goals as realistic? Do you periodically give them feedback on how effective they are in advancing toward the goals? Do you help your groups—committees, task forces, project teams—to set goals as a group?

Delegating

What are you now doing that one or more of your subordinates could do? If some tasks are too complicated for a single subordinate, could you form a group to work on them? What tasks or functions could you delegate that subordinates would see as an opportunity to grow and advance? What responsibilities could you delegate to certain employees that they would regard as a reward for their proven performance?

Rewarding

Are you consistent about rewarding your employees when they have performed as you expected them to perform? Do you make it clear that you reward individual performance that contributes to the success of the whole group—collaboration, support, peer mentoring, and so forth? When a group performs in your department, do you reward people for their contributions to the success of the group? Do your employees all realize that when they turn in good performance, it will be recognized—always?

Questions to Help You Determine Your Action Plan

- What can you do that you are not now doing or are not doing as much as you can?
- Who will be affected?
- Who can be resources to you and to their coworkers?
- How can you initiate the action that you should take? When?

The ratio of we's to I's is the best indicator of the development of a team.

—LEWIS D. EIGEN CEO, SOCIAL AND HEALTH SERVICES, LTD.

THE TEAM LEADER AS FACILITATOR

If you are a manager, you're familiar with the traditional roles of the boss. You plan, direct, assign, control, guide, organize—all those functions you know so well. But you may be less familiar with the role of facilitator. Facilitating a group means what the word says: You make it easier for the group to do its work. The emphasis, of course, is on the group. You subordinate your role as manager to that of facilitator. The group becomes the important entity.

Subordinating the managerial role is sometimes difficult for managers. They believe they are surrendering their managerial prerogatives. They may also view the group suspiciously, as if it could become competitive with the manager. It's a give-and-take situation: As manager, you give up a bit to gain quite a bit more. A well-developed and effective team can give you higher productivity and greatly significant results. The team gets glory, but so do you for having had the wisdom and skill to bring the group along to a high level of effectiveness.

As facilitator, you do not surrender control, as some mangers fear. You are there as a part of the proceedings. You can intervene when the group seems to go awry or to exceed whatever authority and mandate you've given it. But if you are comfortable with being a facilitator rather than a director or prime mover, your reward will probably be a seasoned, competent, reliable group of people who will take initiative, assume ownership, and recognize strong motivating forces within themselves.

The consequences of not taking on the role of facilitator are great: You and your team can become a dysfunctional group. Here is what you can expect:

- Ignorance of or low commitment to imposed goals leads to minimal performance.
- Rewards have little or no motivational value because employees believe they are based on subjective factors, prejudice, and personal preference.
- People avoid unrequired helping of others, and they show a that's-your-problem mentality.
- Few ideas or suggestions for improvement are contributed, because employees say, "What's the use? Who listens to me?"
- Decisions are forced by majority vote, often without a full consideration of options or circumstances, and they frequently have to be altered or remade.
- Conflicts create walls between employees and subgroups so that cooperation is difficult or nonexistent.
- Competition is keen, and employees are sometimes willing to undermine the effectiveness of others to gain advantage.

A FACILITATOR'S CHECKLIST

☐ As a facilitator, I accept the reality that my primary responsibility is to help the group achieve its objectives rather than to lead it.

☐ I realize that a group, given a responsibility and some authority, may achieve its objectives in ways and with methods that are different from what I might choose.

☐ I know that the group may make mistakes, but I also recognize that I must give group members a certain freedom to make mistakes so that they can learn from them.

☐ It's important to encourage the team to deal with conflicts among members in its own way, without premature interference from me.

☐ I realize that the group must come to its own solutions when it has problems, and that imposing my solution on it may be detrimental to the effectiveness of the group as it seeks to improve its working.

☐ When I see ways that I believe can improve the way the team works, I recognize that I should offer advice in the form of suggestions to be considered by the group.

☐ I have to have tolerance for the group's disagreement with me as to the helpfulness of my advice as facilitator.

☐ I remind myself that in most cases, emphasizing the positive behaviors and influences in the group has a team-building impact that is greater than if I frequently criticize the team's mistakes or floundering.

☐ When I sharply disagree with opinions voiced in the group, I am careful to give the contributors enough time and attention to ensure that I really do understand the points they are making.

☐ The group processing that the team members do is probably a greater learning experience for them than what I might say about the process.

☐ I realize that my interactions with team members constitute a model for them.

☐ It's helpful for group members when I periodically communicate their progress and achievements to them.

☐ When I see effective performance in the group, I know that my pointing it out and praising it can have an impact on the motivation of the team members.

☐ I am conscious that my facial expressions, body language, and gestures can communicate negative messages to the group.

☐ One of the best rewards I can hand the group is to praise its progress and achievement to higher management.

- People often work with insufficient knowledge of standards and goals; sometimes they even assume incorrect goals and standards.
- People seek power to build influential subgroups that may contribute nothing to the success of the entire work group.
- Morale is low or nonexistent.
- There is a pervasive belief that "you do what you have to do to get by."
- Informal employee groups exist to thwart the aims of management.

INTERGROUP RELATIONS

As team leader, you act as liaison with other groups outside your team, either on the same level or higher. The last thing in the world you want to create is competition with other groups and suspicion in higher management as to what your successful team is doing. And you want the members of your team to have confidence that you will represent their best interests. Here are a few suggestions.

Pitfalls to Avoid

- *Keep praise and publicity proportionate.* Give credit where it is due, but be careful not to seem to be using the team as your vehicle to glory. Let others know what the group is working on and what it has accomplished. Keep management informed of progress. If the team has a remarkable achievement under its belt, you don't have to keep quiet. But keep the terms of publicity confined to what you can report on objectively.

Stay in tune with the culture in your organization, which can guide you as to how much you can publicize without creating adverse reaction.

• *Don't be the sole conduit to higher management.* Granted, it's primarily your job to report to higher management and to relay management decisions and policies back to the group, but share your responsibilities. Let the group prepare progress reports for the higher levels, and invite top management to come in to talk with the team as a whole.

• *Emphasize intergroup collaboration.* Groups can get very chummy—so much so that they become closed communities. Make it clear to team members that you value their working well together with people from other departments and teams. There must be no "us versus them" in their dealings with other members of the organization. You may even look for opportunities to offer the resources of your team to other functional units.

Sometimes you may have to protect the team against outside interference. People from top management or other departments will consult with members of your team to get information or to ask them to take on special assignments. You have to be prepared to impress upon these people that as team leader, you act as go-between. Tell your team members to come to you or refer questions and assignments to you if they are approached by those who, strictly speaking, should not be approaching them.

CHAPTER 4

THE IMPORTANCE OF PARTICIPATIVE MANAGEMENT

Participation in an organization means that people who are affected by or involved in a decision have a voice in making it. The decisions they make may involve problem solving, work scheduling, task assignment, training, or any number of issues that relate to the effectiveness of their operation. People participate in setting goals and in evaluating one another's performance. They may even decide how rewards are distributed. Whatever the decision, the underlying reality is that employees share leadership with their bosses.

This does not necessarily mean that all organizations practicing participative management are democratic. Not everyone has an equal vote. It's possible that not all decisions are voted on. What is likely is that everyone has the privilege of trying to influence the decision-making process when the decision affects him or her. At the very least, employees in a participative environment are confident that management does not knowingly and arbitrarily make decisions that are contrary to the welfare of employees.

In a shared leadership situation, the relationship between management and employees is based on trust, respect, and openness.

Some managers believe that such sharing indicates an abdication of management rights and responsibilities. It's an easy way out for managers who want to let go of their obligations, they say. But achieving participation by employees is not easy. It sometimes takes a long time for people to develop the trust and credibility that are necessary for participative management to work. It's a nurturing process. But as mentioned earlier, the results, sometimes long in coming, can be seen in deepened employee commitment, increased motivation, and greater productivity.

One of the best-known proponents of participative management was the social scientist Rensis Likert, who was director of the Institute for Social Research at the University of Michigan. It was Likert's conviction, based on years of research in organizations, that better decisions come out of participation and that people who make those decisions are more highly committed to carrying them out than those not involved in the process. He published his research in two books—*New Patterns of Management* (1961) and *The Human Organization* (1967)—where he defined four management systems: (1) Exploitative Authoritative, (2) Benevolent Authoritative, (3) Consultative, and (4) Participative Group. Here's a description of the first three:

1. *Exploitative Authoritative*. Management does not trust subordinates, whose opinions are not sought in setting policy and making decisions. Motivation comes from fear, threats, and occasionally rewards. Communication flows chiefly downward. What comes upward tends to be inaccurate, representing mainly what employees think management wants to hear. Goals are set from on high.

2. *Benevolent Authoritative*. Management and employees exist in a master-servant relationship. The system includes some involvement of employees, more rewards than in System 1, and slightly better upward communication. This is a paternalistic organization—not unfriendly, as is System 1, but without much concern for employee satisfaction.

3. *Consultative*. Management keeps control of things but might consult employees before arriving at decisions or solutions to problems. Communication upward is better, but employees are still cautious about what they send up. Unpleasant or unfavorable information is not freely offered. Employees realize that their input on decisions may not be taken seriously.

Likert demonstrated that he was far from being alone in his belief that participation breeds more effective organizations. The vast majority of people he interviewed, both managers and

All for one, one for all.

—ALEXANDRE DUMAS FRENCH PLAYWRIGHT AND NOVELIST

subordinates, also believed that their organizations functioned better when leadership was shared, when communication flowed freely, when employees could join in the goal-setting processes, and when subordinates helped make the decisions that affected them. Likert argued that the closer the organization was to what he called System 4 (Participative Group), the more effective it was. Here's a description of System 4:

4. *Participative Group*. Management trusts employees and regards them as willingly working toward the achievement of organizational objectives. People are motivated by rewards. At all levels, employees are involved in discussing and deciding those issues that are important to them. Communication is quite accurate and goes up, down, and across. Goals are not ordered from on high; rather, they are set with the participation of the people who will work to achieve them. Because information flows freely in all directions, management knows what it needs to function. And people on lower levels realize how important it is that management be apprised of everything that goes on. Management doesn't feel that letting go of data is tantamount to surrendering power and status.

CHAPTER 5

THE STAGES IN BUILDING A TEAM

A common fiction among managers is that to get a team, you bring together a number of people (preferably compatible with one another), let them work and meet together, and behold— you have a team. Actually, a team develops in stages, over a period of time.

STAGE 1: SEARCHING

The initial phase in the formation of a new group is often characterized by confusion over the roles that each person will play, the task to be performed, the type of leadership, and where the leadership will come from. (There may be a formally constituted leader, but most members are aware that others in the group will play leadership roles as well.) People have been assigned to the group, but they see themselves primarily as individuals. The group is still a gathering of persons.

Stage 1 is searching time: "What are we here for?" "What part shall I play?" "What am I supposed to do?" With the confusion you can also expect to find anxiety, even anger, and almost certainly dependence on a leader. When roles and tasks are unclear, people experience anxious feelings. They may be angry because they have been thrust into an unfamiliar setting without clear directions on how to deal with it. The interactions between people at this stage reflect relationships, biases, perceptions, and antagonisms brought in from outside the group. The roles that people initially experiment with in the new group situation usually resemble those they have performed outside the group. They are just on the threshold of searching for a new identity: their group role.

STAGE 2: DEFINING

The second stage involves a definition of the task to be performed, or the objective to be reached, by the group. People begin to see what kinds of roles they want to play in reaching the objective. They tend to see themselves as individuals working with other individuals to perform a task. They are not yet a true group, but rather a collection of persons brought together for a common purpose.

Certain predictable interactions emerge. Conflicts may occur between those who want to get the job done quickly and those who want to proceed more deliberately. Clashes may also arise between those who have already decided on how the job should get done and those of a more experimental bent. Some people insist on applying solutions they brought in to the project, while others worry about whether the problem or issue has been defined correctly. There are usually members who want a strong, autocratic direction from the outset, and others who prefer to work in a more democratic, open atmosphere.

The path to greatness is along with others.

—BALTASAR GRACÍAN SPANISH PRIEST

There are usually many personal agendas. Some members want to gain influence in the group, either because they see themselves as natural leaders—as experts in the subject to be discussed—or because they want to see the group adopt their own priorities and methodology. Others want to use the group to increase their own visibility and power. Highly task-oriented members may become impatient with those who wish to pay attention to the group dynamics—what goes on between people.

STAGE 3: IDENTIFYING

Members sense that they are no longer a collection of individuals, each with his or her own objectives and agenda, but actually members of a group working together toward a common goal. Whereas they previously saw themselves in roles that were self-serving, they now define their roles as serving the group. Their old roles have become subordinated to the new ones, which are dedicated to helping the group achieve its objective. People who have been task-oriented now understand that it's necessary to pay attention to the group process—interactions among the members—because it takes a balance of concern between the task and the people performing it to be wholly effective.

Up to this point of coalescence, members have retained individuality or joined subgroups in order to enjoy more influence. The fragmentation fades as people identify with the group. The group takes on a unique personality of its own, just as its members are unique personalities.

STAGE 4: PROCESSING

Not only do members work together on the task or the objective, they evaluate their effectiveness in doing so. They experiment with new roles that will help the group be successful, such as leadership. Formal leadership may become less pronounced as members pass the leadership around. The team members look at how they operate in hopes of developing even more effective ways to reach group goals.

STAGE 5: ASSIMILATING/REFORMING

Groups formed to do a task or project usually die when the work has been completed. There will probably be a period of grief when members mourn the passing of what was a significant, gratifying involvement.

Groups that have a permanent mission change. Some people leave, and others join. There is no dying. For them, the fifth stage is more accurately described as assimilating/reforming. They absorb the new members and close ranks when others leave. New dynamics emerge. From time to time, the group changes its personality as it changes its membership and its tasks.

PART II

HOW PEOPLE WORK EFFECTIVELY IN A TEAM

CHAPTER 6

HELPING TEAM MEMBERS BUILD COMMITMENT

To get the commitment of your people to the objectives you want to achieve, you must understand what they want to get out of their work and their association with you. You need to understand what motivates people at work to do a good job. And the first reality is that you do not and cannot motivate them. We all motivate ourselves and no one else.

There is a motivation theory that provides a universal key to what motivates people to be productive on the job: expectancy theory. It is mainstream psychology; it is simple and practical; and it works. Expectancy theory explains that people, given choices, choose the option that promises to give them the greatest reward. In the simplest terms, when you have, say, three choices, you'll choose the one that provides you with the result you value the most. The theory applies to the career you select, the car you buy, the task you start the day with, what you order for lunch, where you go on vacation, and so on.

However, when you make your choice, you must be reasonably sure that the reward you are looking for can be attainable without undue risk or effort. In short, you must have a reasonable expectation of getting what you want (that's where the expectancy comes in). To illustrate: You shop for a new television. Since you like sports, you'd like to see the games on a wide-screen TV. But when you look at the prices for large sets, you realize that to spend so much money on a new wide-screen set would put your cash position in jeopardy for a time. As much as you want the big screen, you don't like putting yourself at risk. So you settle for a smaller set and a lesser expenditure.

> When a team outgrows individual performance and learns team confidence, excellence becomes a reality.
>
> —JOE PATERNO
> HEAD FOOTBALL COACH, PENN STATE UNIVERSITY

Rewards are very important to people at work. It's a myth that most people work primarily for money. Most people would say that they value interesting work, challenge, and advancement opportunities over money. Actually—and this is an important consideration for managers—there are two areas in which people find value in their work: the achievement of goals that they have set for themselves internally, and the attainment of objectives that their managers provide them. As motivators, the internal rewards are probably more powerful. For example, people may work for achievement and its varied benefits: the satisfaction of accomplishing things, status, self-esteem, and social rewards. Some employees get very turned on by being part of a group of people they like. Growth and advancement are powerful motivators. For most people, it's very appealing to increase skills, competence, and knowledge so that they know they are better at what they do this year than they were last.

As manager, you can take advantage of your employees' internal reward drives if you can help them find a way to achieve their personal goals (such as a sense of achievement) through helping you achieve your organizational goals. For example, you seek to have a team working for you, because you believe that a team can be more productive than an aggregate of individual employees. Some of your employees respond to being part of a group because they have high social needs. The psychologist terms these affiliation needs. These people like to be part of a congenial, successful group, so they find increased motivation in being part of your team.

SELF-ASSESSMENT: WHAT MAKES PEOPLE WORK WELL?

Indicate next to each statement whether you agree with it, disagree with it, or are uncertain.

	Agree	Dis-agree	Uncer-tain
1. People who are motivated to work perform better on the job than those who are not.	☐	☐	☐
2. Some people are unmotivated, and there is nothing the manager can do with them.	☐	☐	☐
3. In general, people won't work at something they don't like to do.	☐	☐	☐
4. The attitudes that a manager has toward subordinates can affect the work they do.	☐	☐	☐
5. Most people work primarily for money.	☐	☐	☐
6. The style of managing plays an important role in employee motivation.	☐	☐	☐
7. Few people welcome criticism of their work.	☐	☐	☐
8. People always seem to want to be rewarded for doing a job.	☐	☐	☐
9. The average employee will not be committed to a task or a job that he or she doesn't find valuable.	☐	☐	☐

(continues)

Self-Assessment (continued)

	Agree	Dis-agree	Uncer-tain
10. A manager can often make work more desirable to an employee.	☐	☐	☐
11. Whether people in a work group are strongly motivated depends largely on the way they are managed.	☐	☐	☐
12. When employees suspect that they will have difficulty doing the work, they usually avoid doing it or else lose motivation.	☐	☐	☐
13. Membership in a team can persuade employees that the work is doable and can increase their expectation of success.	☐	☐	☐
14. Employees who are happy at work perform better than those who are not.	☐	☐	☐
15. Managers have the ability to increase the value of work in employees' eyes as well as their confidence in their ability to do it.	☐	☐	☐

ANALYZING YOUR SELF-ASSESSMENT

1. **Agree.** You didn't have any problem with this, did you? People whose work is not very important over the long run usually do just what they have to do to keep their jobs, and not much more.

2. **Disagree.** There's no such person. Everyone is motivated, but not everyone is automatically motivated to do what

his or her manager wants. The answer for managers is to make the work rewarding and doable.

3. **Uncertain.** Some people work at what they don't like to do—for a time. Then the extra energy required to do something they dislike becomes a price they may not be willing to pay. And they probably won't do the job very well while they do it. People work best at what they like to do.

4. **Agree.** According to research, if you show that you expect your people to do a good job, they are more likely to produce good work than if you expect mediocre performance.

5. **Disagree.** In employee surveys, money is usually fourth or fifth on the list. Most people find challenge, interesting work, growth, and advancement more important than money.

6. **Uncertain.** No one style is effective with everyone. And there are some managers with a "nice" style who get poor results from people. The main thing people look for is a manager who helps them achieve what is important to them through their work. If you wish to have an effective team, however, it does help immensely for you to have a participative style—to be willing to share your leadership.

7. **Disagree.** If criticism is necessary to do the job right, people accept it, even if it is painful. Receiving criticism to correct failings is better than floundering or fumbling, which few people are happy doing. Most people want to be successful at what they do.

8. **Agree.** People do what they feel rewarded for doing. That's human nature.

9. **Agree.** That doesn't mean that people won't do the work. Rather, they won't be committed, and probably, over the long haul, they won't be very good at it.

10. **Agree.** You can increase the value of the work by making it more important to employees.

11. **Agree.** Since you are the key to the motivation of employees, you should have no trouble agreeing that your managing has much to do with the motivation your people feel.

12. **Agree.** Expectation of being successful and enjoying the reward for doing the work are central to motivation. If

employees don't see the job as doable, they won't want to tackle it.

13. **Agree.** In an effective team, peers can supply support and help, both of which can increase employees' confidence that the work is doable.

14. **Uncertain.** Employees who feel rewarded perform better than those who don't. All we know about happy people is that they are happy; they don't always do better work.

15. **Agree.** Managers play a crucial role in promoting employee self-confidence and interest in their work.

When your employees have been successful—have performed well for you—you can then supply the external rewards, such as money, praise, promotion, more interesting work, and the like.

PRESCRIPTION FOR GREATER MOTIVATION

You can build value into people's work, and you can increase their expectation that they can be successful in attaining the rewards they want, by following these five steps based on expectancy theory:

Five Steps for Building Value In to People's Work

1. *Tell people what you expect them to do.* On a regular, periodic basis, tell employees what your goals are as well as your standards of performance. People need goals. There isn't any human activity without them. Don't assume that they know what you want. Tell them as specifically as possible.

2. *Make the work valuable.* When you can, assign people to the kinds of work they like and can do well—work that they regard as valuable to them. Give them work that enables them to achieve their personal goals, such as growth, advancement, self-esteem, professional recognition, status, and the like.

3. *Make the work doable.* Increase employees' confidence that they can do what you expect by training, coach-

ing, mentoring, listening, scheduling, providing resources, and so on.

4. *Give feedback.* When employees try to do what you
   expect, give them feedback on how well they are doing.
   Positive feedback tells them what they need to continue
   doing; criticism helps them correct mistakes.

5. *Reward successful performance.* When employees have
   done what you asked them to do, reward them with
   both monetary and nonmonetary recognition.

EFFECTIVE GOAL-SETTING PRACTICES

☐ I try to have goal-setting sessions at least once a year with
all my employees as individuals, and with each team as
necessary.

☐ When possible, I invite employees to join with me in setting
worthwhile goals for the department.

☐ With employees whose performance is reliable, I often leave
it to them to determine the methods they will use to reach
their goals.

☐ I invite employees to set personal goals for their growth and
advancement.

☐ I try to know what employees want out of their work, and
what their needs and goals are.

☐ Once I have agreed on a goal, I make sure it is addressed.

☐ I let employees know at the time of setting goals how
important they are to me.

☐ I usually incorporate goals in appraisals.

☐ I make sure to find out how realistic the goals are to
employees who are charged with reaching them.

☐ I make sure periodically that all employees understand not
only my goals but the performance standards I expect of
them.

CHAPTER 7

TEAM-BUILDING ROLES

In an effectively functioning team, members consistently perform certain roles that contribute not only to reaching the current objectives set by the group but also to the ongoing improvement in the team's long-term operation. Some of the most common and helpful team-building roles include supporting, confronting, gatekeeping, mediating, harmonizing, summarizing, and process observing. This chapter looks at each role in detail.

SUPPORTING

Supporting another member of the team goes beyond reinforcing the other's point of view when you agree with it. That's immensely desirable, but even more important is providing support and encouragement for a team member when you may not agree with him or her. In the latter function, your support says, "I know that your idea or opinion is something you take seriously, and I accept that seriousness even though I may not have the same view." But over the long-term life of the group, you realize that your support and encouragement of another member result in more and better contributions from him or her, if only because that member realizes that his or her comments will be accepted and considered, and not put down or discounted.

CONFRONTING

There are times when a person's behavior is detrimental to the success of the team as it works toward its goals. (See Chapter

8.) The "offender" may try to keep others from offering their ideas, may publicly make fun of the contributions, or may say unkind words about another person that have nothing to do with the inherent value of his or her contributions. In such an instance, another team member may confront the undesirable behavior: "Ted, it bothers me that you break in with your own arguments without letting Sheila finish. I'd really like to hear her out before you respond." Or "Randy, I don't think it's fair to suggest that Jerry's opposition to your idea is based on his 'stubbornness,' as you describe it."

Confronting is a constructive role when it is confined to people's behavior. When one member confronts another's personality, or presumed attitudes or motives, the result is usually disruption of the group's work and resentment in the person who is being confronted.

GATEKEEPING

Some members of a team are less assertive, and others far more so. Consequently, some opinions from the somewhat retiring people get ignored; they may not even be expressed. When the gate seems closed to some contributors, a team member performs as gatekeeper: "Hey, Jenny has been trying to make a point for the past ten minutes, but she hasn't gotten more than two or three words in. I'd like for the rest of us to stop talking long enough to hear what she has to say." Or "I'm distressed that we keep talking about 'Phil's idea,' when I distinctly remember that Ruth made the same point two days ago."

There are times when certain members monopolize a discussion so completely that others can't enter it or are intimidated enough to keep silent. In this case, a member might say to the monopolizers, "You folks have expressed yourselves quite clearly. I'd like to hear what some of the others feel. For example, Ben looks as if he has something to say."

MEDIATING

Sometimes disputes can be so intense or prolonged that the people involved no longer listen or respond to each other.

They may have become so polarized that they can't move toward each other's point of view. One member who is not involved in the debate intervenes, not to arbitrate but to illuminate. First, the member asks permission to interpret each position, then does so for each side of the argument. After each interpretation, the mediating member asks whether that version reflects the disputant's argument. The arguer has a chance to revise or correct. The intervention can clarify the real differences and areas of agreement that neither side has heard. It also provides a chance for others in the group to discuss the disputed points. Groups can get quite stuck during a debate; mediating can break the stall and push the discussion forward.

HARMONIZING

Again, during a heavy debate-style disagreement, the disputants can become so involved in scoring points for themselves that they fail to realize their agreement on certain points. Perhaps they simply use different terms. An intervenor summarizes the various views to show how close they actually are. Then he or she invites other members of the team to help the debaters build on the areas of agreement that they have not listened to during the intense discussion.

I do not resent criticism, even when, for the sake of emphasis, it parts for the time with reality.

—WINSTON CHURCHILL BRITISH PRIME MINISTER, 1940—1945 AND 1951—1955

SUMMARIZING

A group can find itself awash in details or varying points of view, and the consequence is confusion. Members begin to ask, "Where are we?" or "What are we talking about?" At times the members of the group are stuck, feeling that there are simply too many pieces of a jigsaw puzzle before them. One member intervenes to sum up the discussion so far. The summarizing gives the group time to breathe. And a good summary clarifies some of the confusion. Furthermore, the summary may restore the group's confidence in itself by showing that more progress has been made than anyone previously thought. The summary also provides concrete points on which further work can be based.

PROCESS OBSERVING

In any group effort, the goal is essential. It's the content of any discussion and the basis for any assignments of group resources. The methodology is equally vital: for example, whether the group is to work as an entire entity or break up into smaller segments as needed. Techniques of organizing and reporting are other examples of methodology. But there is a third aspect of a team's work, which is sometimes neglected: its process—that is, the dynamics of the group, what goes on between the members of the team. Are there power or control issues among the members? Does the group frequently avoid tackling major issues? A process observer may say, "In the past half hour, we've had two proposals put on the table, and neither has really been addressed. Why can't we deal with them?" Or "I'm feeling frustrated, because everyone is interrupting everyone else. No one gets to finish a statement, and I'm wondering why." Or "It's strange that we keep talking about the advertising program for the new product line, and that has nothing to do with our work."

The process observer forces the group to look at how it is functioning—something that the group might not have done otherwise, if only because it was so involved in the details that it couldn't see the whole picture.

Processing is not an entirely negative function. When the group works effectively, it finds feedback helpful on what it is doing correctly, so members can repeat the constructive behavior.

THE VALUE OF LISTENING

One other role is essential to the success of any group: listening. At all times, every member of the group needs to be aware of how important it is to hear what people are saying. Unfortunately, listening takes concentration and commitment. It can be hard work. Most people don't listen well. They have to train themselves to do so. They become so absorbed with their own agendas and viewpoints that they aren't open to those of others. They become defensive when their comments and

(Text continues on page 45.)

IDENTIFYING GROUP-BUILDING BEHAVIORS

Read the following statements made by participants in a group discussion, and identify each as one of the following group-building behaviors:

a: Supporting
b: Confronting
c: Gatekeeping
d: Mediating
e: Harmonizing
f: Summarizing
g: Process observing

1. "Ralph, you've given us a lot of your ideas in the last ten minutes, and I wonder whether we can take time out from your presentation to get some other opinions or reactions." _____

2. "Twice I've heard someone suggest that we get the thinking of our supervisors on the proposed procedures, but the suggestion hasn't been picked up on for some reason. I think it's an important idea that should be discussed, not passed over." _____

3. "I'm not sure I completely understand all the points you've been making, Joe and Connie. Maybe it would help me, and others, if I fed back to you what I've been hearing, and you can tell me whether I'm right." _____

4. "Quite candidly, Jim, I hadn't thought of that as being a problem before you mentioned it. I'm glad you brought it up so we can look at it." _____

5. "We've talked about so many things that maybe this is a good time to look at all of the ideas that have been offered. It would help me to organize things in my mind." _____

6. "Joan, you and Petra seem to differ on the time period, but you both seem to agree that it should be short term. Am I right?" _____

7. "I know it looks as if we're talking about a cat and dog from every town, but what surprises me is that there seem to be certain threads running through the discussion so far. May I review what I've written down, and the rest of you can tell me whether I've captured the various comments accurately?" _____

8. "I haven't heard anyone finish a statement in the last fifteen minutes. Everyone seems to be interrupting everyone else." _____

9. "Donna, every time someone makes a suggestion, you say that's been tried before. I think you ought to give us a chance to judge whether the idea being proposed today is really the same as before, or maybe different. Or whether circumstances are different." _____

10. "I counted four times that Earl tried to get a word in, but no one let him. I'd like to hear what's on his mind, and I think we ought to give him a chance." _____

11. "That's an interesting approach, Harry. I'm not sure it would work, but I think we ought to look at it." _____

12. "So that I'm more confident that I understand what each of you is talking about, let me tell you what I hear you saying, and you check me out. Okay?" _____

13. "Apparently the bottom line of what you're both saying is that we have to cut that division back. But you don't seem to agree on how and when. Let's work backward from that to see just where you may be parting company." _____

14. "What I don't understand is why Mary and Eddie are doing all the talking about this. Is it because we're not interested? Should we be talking about something else? What's going on now doesn't seem to be helpful to us." _____

opinons are challenged, and defensiveness is not conducive to open-mindedness and objectivity. And if people hear what they'd rather not hear, they can become so emotional that their listening shuts down.

Paul makes a critical remark about the direction of a discussion, and immediately Virginia rebuts with a comment about Paul's remark that bears little resemblance to what he said. John intervenes: "Virginia, that's not what I heard Paul say. Am I right, Paul?" John may wish to describe what he heard Paul say, so as to make it easier for Virginia to listen.

A lot of group time is wasted when people respond to what they think they heard without checking to make sure that what they think they heard is actually the meaning of the speaker. Rather than jumping in with a rebuttal or a criticism, try saying, "What I heard you say is. . . . Am I correct?" Checking is so easy, and it saves a lot of time and energy.

ANSWERS

1. **c:** Gatekeeping
2. **b/g:** Confronting/ process observing
3. **d:** Mediating
4. **a:** Supporting
5. **f:** Summarizing
6. **e:** Harmonizing
7. **f:** Summarizing
8. **g:** Process observing
9. **b:** Confronting
10. **c:** Gatekeeping
11. **a:** Supporting
12. **d:** Mediating
13. **e:** Harmonizing
14. **g:** Process observing

PTER 8

SUBVERTING ROLES

hat does not operate as effectively as it can, you
ople performing roles that apparently suit their
ut act against the group's interests. The roles are
ctive, undermining the chances that the group can
eam. The principal obstructive functions that you'll
tting off, analyzing or labeling, dominating, yes-
d naysaying. Let's examine each in detail so that
ognize them and deal with them when you encoun-
nong team members.

NG OFF

ig. Suddenly, Craig says, "Hey, that reminds me of
Do you remember when? . . ." Jeff is probably
e with his mouth open, a quizzical look on his face.
hut him off—has silenced him. In this case, Craig
off in a different conversational direction, but he
have started to rebut Jeff's point before Jeff finished.
it have used derisive humor: "Good old predictable
scussion is complete until Jeff talks about that bad
xperience he had a couple of years back." Everyone
it least smiles, and Jeff's usefulness is destroyed for
it.

e shutting-off method is for other members in the
to ignore the speaker. For example, a member says,
ought to determine the best way to spend the next
half hour talking about the project. How do we proceed? How
do we organize ourselves?" The person is ignored. It's as if no
one heard him. He sits there feeling a bit foolish. In some

groups, ignoring one another is standard practice: Someone asks a question or makes a suggestion, and the discussion continues as though nothing has been said by this member.

When some people are silenced, they get angry and break in to complain, often starting an argument. Others withdraw, saying to themselves, "What's the point of trying to make a contribution?" Still others resolve to create barriers, tit for tat, when their interrupters offer an idea or make a comment: "You get me, I'll get you."

ANALYZING OR LABELING

When you put labels on a person's behavior, or you try to describe his or her attitudes or motives, you're threatening a discussion. Martha has been arguing a particular point of view, and she has met some disagreement. She begins to talk forcefully, dominating the conversation. Finally, Shelly says, "I think, Martha, if you weren't being so defensive, we could probably approach this more constructively." Instantly Martha denies that she has acted out of defensiveness.

In another case, Jan returns to a subject that has been mentioned a number of times: cutting back people in another section. Mark reacts vigorously and negatively, whereupon Jan retorts, "I don't know, Mark, why you are so threatened by talking about this cutback. It's not going to affect you." Mark responds with a denial that his resistance is based on feeling threatened.

In yet a third example, Rob protests when a coworker, Priscilla, criticizes a third member of the group, Cal. Priscilla turns on Rob with the charge "You always try to protect Cal, and I'm getting tired of it. It's like you don't want people to talk about him, that you're trying to hide something about him."

In these three cases, someone is putting a label on behavior or suggesting that another group member has a particular attitude or unworthy motive. A label or analysis can easily sidetrack a discussion while people argue whether the label or the analysis is justified. The give-and-take easily degenerates into "I didn't," "You did," "I wasn't," "You were," "I'm right," "You're wrong." Dead end.

DOMINATING

The dominator likes to take over the discussion. He or she may rationalize, "I'm a person who likes to get things done, so let's cut through all this nonsense and get our act together," or "We're really wasting time. I say we should vote on this and move on."

The dominator wants influence and can be very heavy-handed in efforts to get it. The problem for the group is that the dominator is usually less interested in the goals of the group and far more focused on his or her personal agendas. When the dominator takes over, other people's participation falls off. The group doesn't get the full value of its resources.

YES-BUTTING

Probably one of the most common behaviors in a group discussion is the yes-but response. For example, "Yes, I understand what you're saying, but I think you're missing the point." Translated: "I hear you, but you're wrong." Sometimes people use the yes-but technique to try to soften the blow of disagreement: "I agree that that's an excellent idea, but I don't think it'll work here." Consider that if the idea won't work, it's hardly excellent. The yes-but technique displays hypocrisy at worst, and a personal discounting of the other person at best. Very often, what the contributor hears is "I know you think you've come up with a good idea, but it really isn't worth much."

The yes-but approach can be used so skillfully that it's hard to detect. To illustrate: "I believe that Mike has shown his usual imaginative approach in coming up with this suggestion, and I think he merits the congratulations of every member of the group for the quality of his thinking, which we've come to expect. However, when you look at the plan closely, you can see a slight flaw that is all too easy to overlook but that could render the whole idea unworkable."

Discussions among group members are most effective when they communicate in clear, unambiguous messages. The yes-but response seems to say one thing when it actually says another.

NAYSAYING

In many groups, there is the person who declares himself or herself the "devil's advocate," whose function it is to make sure that whatever is bad about another person's idea gets expressed. So relentless can such naysayers be in emphasizing what is wrong that what is right can get buried. The discussion becomes lopsided.

Unfortunately, *no* has a power that is disproportionate in many deliberations. If the group members are exploring an option that may be risky, is unpleasant, or at least carries uncertain consequences, they may be unusually susceptible to the naysayer, who provides them with a reason not to proceed further: "I really don't think we have enough information on this. Let's table this." Or "We tried something like this a few years ago, and it didn't work." Or "We need to go slowly on this, because if we make a misstep, we could pay through the nose." With a collective sigh of relief, the group abandons the discussion. For the moment, the naysayer has opened up the escape hatch.

There are ways to neutralize or reverse the damage of behaviors that are obstructive. The simplest is to immediately intervene by using one or more of these countering statements:

Countering Team-Subverting Behaviors

"I've heard what you have to say about the project, Eileen, but I'd also like to hear what others around the table feel. Would you please just withhold your comments for a time, and let's hear from others."

"I really am not interested in why Sam may have been impelled psychologically to take that position. I'm sure he has good reasons, and those are what I'd like to hear."

"Yes, I agree that there may be reasons why this won't work, but I'm intrigued by the possibility that it will. At the moment, I'd like to hear why it just might."

(Text continues on page 52.)

IDENTIFYING TEAM-SUBVERTING BEHAVIORS

Read the following statements made by participants in a group discussion, and identify each as one of the following team-subverting behaviors:

a: Shutting off
b: Analyzing or labeling
c: Dominating
d: Yes-butting
e: Naysaying

1. "We're talking in circles. Here's what we really need to do: bite the bullet and tell those people that this is the way it's going to be done. It's the only thing to do. Otherwise we're going to be here forever. I say we take a vote on it right now so we can get on to more productive things."   _____

2. "Swen, I think you've made an extraordinary point, and if the circumstances were a bit different, it would be the solution we've been looking for. Unfortunately, I don't think that what you're sug- gesting has taken into sufficient consideration the fact that we don't have such a skilled person on our staff."   _____

3. "Come on, Rita, now you're projecting."   _____

4. "If you'll look in the files, you'll see that we did that, and it didn't work then. How come we think it'll work now? I think we ought to look elsewhere. We're wasting our time on this direction."   _____

5. "Hey, I'm just reporting some facts. There's no need for you to get angry."   _____

6. "I think those issues you're talking about are marginal. A more important consideration is whether we can meet the deadline."   _____

7. "Can we keep all the emotional stuff out of the talk? Let's keep our heads."   _____

8. "I suggest that this discussion is premature. Why don't we wait until we have more facts?"   _____

9. "That just won't work."   _____

10. "This discussion is way off the track. Let's get back to the Protax project. That makes more sense."   _____

(continues)

Team-Subverting Behaviors (continued)

11. "I want to pick up on the point that Tom made, because I think it is important, although I really believe it would be more relevant in slightly different terms. What you said, Tom, is timely, but I think it needs to be reworded and rethought." _____

12. "You know, Midge, every time we bring up anything that even remotely has to do with the decision to add bonuses to the field compensation system, you seem to get uptight. Why do you feel the need to protect the old system? You're certainly doing everything to sabotage any possible change." _____

"Okay, now that the two of you have talked at length, I'm well-acquainted with where you stand. Here's what I think, and then I hope others will join in."

"Well, maybe it didn't work then, but perhaps times have changed. I wonder whether this idea is now facing a different world. Could someone else comment?"

"I don't know whether Rita is projecting or not, and I guess I don't care. Rita, please elaborate on your thinking."

"Wait a minute. You may think these issues are not important, but I'd like to give Egan a chance to show us they are. Go ahead, Egan."

"You didn't let Ray continue. I want to hear the rest of his thoughts. Go ahead, Ray."

ANSWERS

1. **c:** Dominating
2. **d:** Yes-butting
3. **b:** Analyzing or labeling
4. **e:** Naysaying
5. **b:** Analyzing or labeling
6. **a:** Shutting off
7. **b:** Analyzing or labeling
8. **e:** Naysaying
9. **e:** Naysaying
10. **c:** Dominating
11. **d:** Yes-butting
12. **b:** Analyzing or labeling

PART

COMMUNICATION AND CONFLICT IN A TEAM

CHAPTER 9

COMMUNICATING IN A TEAM

PROFILE OF ASSERTIVE COMMUNI- CATORS

Assertive communicators share the following characteristics:

- They believe that they have the right to express their needs, wants, and wishes to their coworkers.

- When they are in conflict or disagreement with others, they assume that those others, generally, are willing to join in the search for agreement or a solution.

- They express themselves when they are angry or distressed.

- They take steps to change conditions they don't like or to persuade others to change them.

(Continued)

There can't be collaboration and support without communication among the people in a group. The way people communicate with one another—in both words and nonverbal clues—not only reflects how they feel about working with one another but also builds (or detracts from) the team's effectiveness. Good communication gives clear messages, which are conducive to people working productively and harmoniously, without misunderstanding and misinterpretation. As people on the team learn to take other members at face value, they build trust and credibility. The twin messages are (1) what you see is what is there and (2) what you hear is what is meant. The "Spectrum of Communication" chart shows the whole range of communicating styles: The extremes of aggressiveness and nonassertiveness are at each end.

One of the most helpful forms of communication training developed in recent years is what we've labeled assertiveness training. Many people have gone through assertiveness training, which has helped them to identify their needs and wants and to communicate those needs and wants in a manner that others find acceptable. Assertive communication generally clarifies the meaning of people's statements and avoids common communication pitfalls that arouse resentment, hurt, and defensiveness.

When combined with responsive communication, assertiveness can become tool for negotiation, problem solving, and conflict resolution. The assertiveness-responsiveness (A-R) approach is the optimum method of communicating. It acknowledges the rights and feelings of each person in a transaction, creates a

55

dialogue in which each person feels comfortable expressing feelings about what is going on, and recognizes that each person has needs, wants, and resources. The A–R approach can be used to find an outcome that is acceptable to everyone. Take a look at assertiveness and responsiveness side by side:

- In a conflict situation, they deal with the issues rather than the personalities of the disputants.
- They regard themselves as experts on their feelings and perceptions and regard others as experts on theirs.
- They are accustomed to receiving trust and respect from others.
- They allow ample time for a person with whom they have a problem to express his or her feelings, and they encourage that person to do so, even when the person is hostile to them.
- They believe that consistent assertive behavior establishes them as credible and trustworthy.
- They understand that they convey their assertiveness not only with words but also with gestures and facial expressions that are congruent with the words.

Characteristics of Assertive and Responsive Communication

Assertiveness	Responsiveness
The assertive person:	The responsive person:
Gives information—describes the situation as he or she views it.	*Seeks information*—invites the other person to describe the situation as he or she sees it.
Expresses feelings—relates how he or she feels about what is going on.	*Seeks to know the feelings of the other*—asks the other to describe how he or she feels about the situation and accepts that person without necessarily agreeing.
Seeks change in the other—describes the behavior that he or she would rather see in the other.	*Seeks change in self*—agrees to change his or her own behavior when it has not been helpful or effective.
Defines benefits of the change—delineates the benefits that will accrue to the other person as a result of the change.	*Defines the benefits of the change for oneself*—describes the reward (possibly for both parties) if the desired change is made.

The Spectrum of Communication

Aggressiveness	Assertiveness	Responsiveness	Nonassertiveness
Totally you, excluding others. Disregards the rights and dignity of others. Aggressive statements put down, embarrass, and humiliate.	Primarily you, secondarily others. Expression of your needs and wants in a manner acceptable to others. Can convey unpleasant information in a nonthreatening, nonabrasive manner.	Primarily others, secondarily you. Recognizes that others bring strengths, resources, and differing perceptions to a situation. Seeks to enlist those qualities in meeting joint concerns or solving problems.	Totally others, excluding you. Nonassertiveness is abdication of responsibility and a surrender of rights. Practically invites other people to disregard or take advantage of the nonassertive person.

IDENTIFYING MODES OF COMMUNICATION

Try your hand at identifying the various modes of behavior and communication. Mark each statement as follows:

ag: Aggressive
as: Assertive
r: Responsive
ar: Assertive-responsive
na: Nonassertive

1. "Fred, throughout this whole meeting you have interrupted me time after time, and I'm getting very frustrated and angry. Please stop doing it. Let me finish, and I can relax long enough to listen to you." _____

2. "Hey, Amy, wake up and smell the coffee. I just covered that point a few minutes ago. Were you asleep?" _____

3. "I'm really getting sick and tired of your snide remarks. I don't know what makes you think you can walk in here and act as if you are better than everyone else. Frankly, I think you'd benefit by closing your mouth and opening your ears. But then again, you just might learn something, and that might be scary." _____

4. "You keep asking the same question, Jeff. I gave you the answer when you first asked it, and then again, and now a third time. It's awfully upsetting to me to think that I'm not expressing myself clearly, and if I'm not, I'm wasting everyone's time. So tell me what you have been hearing me say. I guess you must be frustrated, because you keep trying to find out the same information." _____

5. "Yes, I know that I haven't spoken up, but I'm getting the suspicion that you all know so much more about the subject than I do, so I'm just not going to waste your time by telling you what you probably already know." _____

6. "Alan, excuse me for interrupting your conversation with Pete, but I can't help noticing that you often get involved in side conversations when someone else in the meeting is talking. What you're doing distracts me, and I can't concentrate. It impresses me as being very rude. I don't know how you feel about it. Perhaps you don't mean to be disruptive. But I wish you'd show more courtesy when others are speaking to the group. It would be much fairer." _____

7. "I'd be very much interested in what Jan thinks about Perry's comment, especially since Jan looked into this question some months back. Jan, you're being silent. Does that mean that you agree or disagree? Are you just being tactful?"   _____

8. "Frankly, Jim, I don't know what in the world you're talking about. It seems to me that you're just talking and talking and going in circles. I wish you'd get to the point. I don't know why it seems so difficult for you to come out and say what you mean in less than a thousand words."   _____

9. "This discussion is going all over the map. At first I was frustrated, but now I'm just bored. Do others here have the same reaction to what's going on? If you do, what can we do to get more focus into this discussion? I hate to sit here thinking I could better spend my time at my desk."   _____

10. "You're right. I am uncharacteristically quiet. The truth is that I'm sitting here boiling over at what Glen said to me a few minutes ago. Glen, I don't think you were fair to me when you suggested that I'm trying to take credit for some work that my predecessor did. And I can't get with what's going on here as long as I keep hearing your words."   _____

Answers

1. **as:** Assertive.
2. **ag:** Aggressive. The statement is potentially embarrassing.
3. **ag:** Aggressive. The retort is a put-down. Aggressive statements often impute unpleasant attitudes and motives, as with this suggestion that the other person believes he or she is better than everyone else.
4. **ar:** Assertive-responsive. The speaker is giving and seeking information.
5. **na:** Nonassertive. The speaker is abdicating and suggesting that he or she has nothing of value to offer.
6. **ar:** Assertive-responsive. The speaker is giving information and opening the door for Alan to respond. Perhaps Alan doesn't think he's being disruptive. The speaker uses the word *rude*, but says it is his or her impression. In other words, "You're coming across to me as rude, but perhaps you don't mean to be."

7. **r:** Responsive. The speaker seeks information about Jan's thoughts and feelings.
8. **ag:** Aggressive. Jim is referred to as being a bit handicapped in regard to his mental ability.
9. **ar:** Assertive-responsive. The speaker wants to know how others in the meeting feel about his or her description of the situation.
10. **as:** Assertive. Perhaps if Glen apologizes or alters his words, the speaker can stop being angry with him and become a contributor again.

EFFECTIVE COMMUNICATION PRACTICES

To build and maintain a team, its members must be willing and able to communicate with one another in ways that reflect openness, trust, and respect. Successful teams insist that team members willingly share timely information about developments occurring throughout the organization, except what is labeled confidential.

It is considered bad form to withhold or ration information that could be useful to team members. Information is seen as empowering the group, not any one member.

Feedback is serious business. Team members must provide each other with feedback about whether their performance enhances the team's performance or impedes it. Feedback should be given immediately and should be confined to behavior.

When people give feedback to others about their emotions or opinions, it should be prefaced with "It's my perception that . . ." or "You impress me as feeling. . . ." Team members should never assume or label without checking to make sure their perceptions and analyses are correct. No one on a team is immune from receiving feedback. In fact, most people welcome feedback, even when it is critical, because they know it helps them develop more effective behavior.

Feedback should not be delivered as a joke, which can contain hidden messages that make fun of someone.

(Text continues on page 62.)

ASSESSING THE COMMUNICATION PRACTICES OF YOUR TEAM

The following statements describe some communication practices that occur in work groups. Answer each statement "yes" or "no" depending on whether the statement applies to practices in your group.

		Yes	No
1.	Unpleasant opinions regarding group members are expressed indirectly through gossip rather than directly, face-to-face.	☐	☐
2.	Feedback between members that is not complimentary is often couched in tactful, diplomatic language.	☐	☐
3.	When members express disagreement with others, they fall into a yes-butting mode.	☐	☐
4.	Unpleasant truths about the group and its members are clothed in humor.	☐	☐
5.	When people are visibly upset, they deny being angry or having strong emotions.	☐	☐
6.	People seem uncomfortable talking with me about my management and how I lead the work group.	☐	☐
7.	In their communication with one another and in meetings, members of the group speak of the importance of being rational.	☐	☐
8.	When people make cutting remarks that are clothed in humor, most people laugh.	☐	☐
9.	There are many joking relationships between members of the group, and it's considered to be a sign of a good sport to take the ribbing.	☐	☐
10.	When members have conflicts, each disputant reinforces his or her position by reminding team members of the other disputants' past mistakes.	☐	☐
11.	Members seem to be embarrassed and nonplussed by any show of emotions.	☐	☐
12.	Much time is taken up uselessly because people misunderstand what others are saying and respond to statements that weren't made.	☐	☐
13.	In problem-solving discussions, we first affix blame, then we talk about how to correct the problems.	☐	☐
14.	When I criticize an employee, I see sullenness in the person.	☐	☐

(continues)

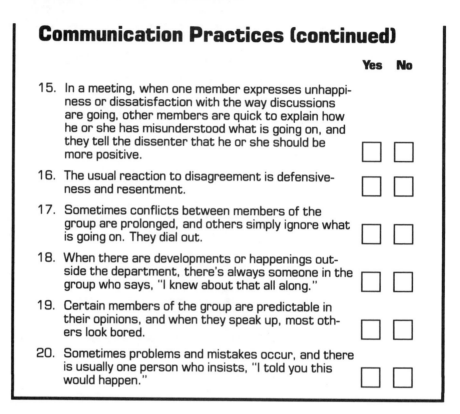

Communication Practices (continued)

	Yes	No
15. In a meeting, when one member expresses unhappiness or dissatisfaction with the way discussions are going, other members are quick to explain how he or she has misunderstood what is going on, and they tell the dissenter that he or she should be more positive.	☐	☐
16. The usual reaction to disagreement is defensiveness and resentment.	☐	☐
17. Sometimes conflicts between members of the group are prolonged, and others simply ignore what is going on. They dial out.	☐	☐
18. When there are developments or happenings outside the department, there's always someone in the group who says, "I knew about that all along."	☐	☐
19. Certain members of the group are predictable in their opinions, and when they speak up, most others look bored.	☐	☐
20. Sometimes problems and mistakes occur, and there is usually one person who insists, "I told you this would happen."	☐	☐

Team members should be encouraged to express their emotions when it is healthy and normal to do so, especially if it will illuminate their perception or perspective on an issue. Aggressiveness and nonassertiveness are not acceptable behaviors in teams. People who dissent or are unhappy with the way the group is working should be supported in what they say, even if other team members do not agree. No one gets "punished" for speaking out. When conflicts between members are prolonged or intense, other team members should step in to help resolve them.

Problem solving means searching for alternatives. It is future-oriented unless there is valuable learning in analyzing the past. People who disagree with a decision or course of action should receive careful attention. They may be telling members something they need to know—they may highlight something no one has considered yet.

Generally, sharing information, providing feedback, and encouraging participation among all team members are the three key communication practices used by successful teams.

ANALYZING YOUR ASSESSMENT

Any one "yes" to the preceding statements indicates a possible impediment to the free flow of information.

When members of the group clothe their comments to one another in tactful language, in humor, or in yes-butting, they avoid candor and honesty. They obscure their messages to make them more palatable. The use of humor among people at work is not always a sign of good, easy, open relationships; instead, it can arise from a perceived need not to be forthright, or perhaps from fear.

A strong insistence on rationality also indicates an uneasiness with openness, even fear. People who deny emotions, in themselves or in others, feel vulnerable. They don't wish to communicate as whole people. In fact, much communication is nonrational—that is, intuitive and emotional.

When people don't listen, they hear what they want to hear and nothing else, so much valuable time is consumed with people not relating to one another. A person may say something and hear a response that sounds as though he or she said something completely different.

Group members whom the preceding statements characterize don't want to take responsibility to help the team work well. A prolonged conflict is a sure sign of such unwillingness. The disputants aren't getting on with their work, and they make it difficult for others to get on with theirs. Yet the conflict is permitted to continue. Team members may simply isolate the arguers and ignore them, just as they do a protester in their midst who criticizes the way the group operates. But people who are isolated are excluded from being full-fledged members of the team.

Others refuse to be full-fledged team members, such as the person who hoards and withholds information. When he or

(Text continues on page 66.)

AN ACTION PLAN FOR ASSERTIVENESS AND ASSERTIVENESS-RESPONSIVENESS

Description of a problem or a need for correction in a team member:

_____

_____

_____

_____

Following are your statements to resolve the problem or to discuss it constructively, covering the eight main elements of A–R:

- A description of what you see going on:

  _____

  _____

  _____

  _____

- What you plan to say to the other person to find out what he or she believes is going on:

  _____

  _____

  _____

  _____

- How you feel about what is going on (what words do you use?):

  _____

  _____

  _____

  _____

- What words you will use to find out how the other person feels about the situation:

  _____

  _____

  _____

  _____

- The change you would be willing to make in yourself, if necessary:

  _____

  _____

  _____

  _____

- The change you would like to see in the other person:

  _____

  _____

  _____

  _____

- The benefits to you in making the change:

  _____

  _____

  _____

  _____

- The benefits to the other person in making the change:

  _____

  _____

  _____

  _____

Date of feedback: _____

(continues)

> Describe change in plan because of information that
> emerged in the feedback session:
>
> _____
>
> _____
>
> _____
>
> _____

she uses it, it's for power or prestige reasons, not necessarily
for the aid of the group. Of course, such people may also
withhold out of anxiety: They're not sure they can tell the boss
things he or she may not wish to hear.

Finger pointing is a scoring game: I make you look bad so I
can look good. It's often competitive. But affixing blame is
also self-protective: If you're at fault, I won't be blamed.

Finally, people who have been allowed to become predictable
and not very useful reflect on the unwillingness and inability
of other members to help them be effective.

CHAPTER 10

DEALING WITH CONFLICT IN A TEAM

Handling conflict in a team successfully has several characteristics:

• *Conflict is considered natural.* Team members assume that conflict, disagreement, and promotion of disparate ideas are bound to occur in vibrant, successful groups. Where there is creativity, there exists the chance of conflict.

• *Conflict is resolved through openness.* Since conflict is natural to the group, it is dealt with in a natural way—through open discussion. In many groups that are not teams, conflicts are suppressed. They fester; they influence people's relationships and interactions with one another; they surface in ways that don't always seem related to the original troubling issues. In a team, members know that conflicts can often sharpen the differences, present additional options, and provide checks and balances.

• *Conflict occurs over issues, not over personalities.* People may be parties to conflict, but they are not the issue. As a team member, you may disagree with another member, but he or she is not the target of innuendo, put-downs, or embarrassment. What count are the issues and the perceptions of those issues, not the personalities involved.

• *Conflict involves a search for alternatives.* Team members don't conduct whodunit-type investigations to try to pin the blame on someone for a problem or a failure. The driving motivation in team problem solving is "We don't like the situation as it is now; what would we prefer as an alternative?"

• *Conflict resolution is present-oriented.* A discussion of the conflict concentrates on what is happening in the group now.

Prior disagreements, conversations that have taken place with others outside the group, and previous behaviors of team members in other situations are not part of the working through of the conflict. What matters is the here and now—what is being said now, in this setting.

  • *Conflict is a group issue.* Disagreements that affect certain team members become issues for the entire group to deal with, because they can affect the working of the entire team. Team members, therefore, don't have to resolve differences on their own. The whole team pitches in to help.

DEALING WITH OPPOSITION TO YOUR IDEAS

One of the most common impediments to communicating freely in a group is the defensiveness of people whose ideas and suggestions are being evaluated and perhaps disagreed with, in whole or in part. You've seen defensive, self-protective behavior many times. You've probably experienced it in yourself on occasion. The pulse quickens, heat and color flood the face, palms sweat, the voice rises in pitch and perhaps in volume. These are very natural reactions when one feels attacked or discounted in any way.

The chief problem with defensiveness is that it usually hampers one's ability to listen and to think through what others are saying. Ideally, when an idea is discussed, its originator believes that what will eventually emerge is an idea that is tested and even strengthened. That's often true unless the group has to spend much of its time debating with the originator, who worries that his or her idea is being mangled, misunderstood, and mutilated.

You can train yourself to deal constructively with resistance and disagreement. Of course, it's much easier to do so when you are a member of a supportive and sympathetic group. But if you believe that your idea can stand the rigors of close and thoughtful examination, follow these five suggestions to help you deal with opposition:

MANAGING CONFLICT

When conflict arises, keep the following in mind:

- The person on the other side of the conflict has a point of view that is just as legitimate and reasonable to him or her as yours is to you.

- The other person may also be uncomfortable about the conflict or disagreement, just as you are.

- The other person is usually willing to accept a solution if you can make it sufficiently attractive. At least he or she can be persuaded to work with you to formulate a resolution of the conflict.

- It is safer and wiser to keep to the issues in any discussion and to avoid arguments that are personal.

- The future is often a more constructive base for discussion than the past. Rather than dwell on what or who caused the conflict, emphasize what can be done to provide a solution or an alternative to the situation that exists now.

1. *Relax.* Easily said, not so easily done. Sit back in your chair. Keep your facial expression attentive. Don't frown. Don't shake your head. When you look relaxed, even though inside you may not be, you look confident. You also invite people to discuss your idea openly. And that's valuable to you, because you learn what the others are thinking. If you wish to rebut their criticism or analysis, you're getting the ammunition to do so. On the other hand, when you're relaxed, your filters are open, and you may actually pick up some valuable tips on how to improve your idea.

2. *Listen.* Maintain eye contact. Again, keep your facial expression attentive, showing that you value what is being said. Remain seated back in your chair. If you lean forward, you may look as if you are about to pounce on the person evaluating your idea. Don't interrupt while others are talking unless it is quite clear to you that they have misconstrued your idea and are wasting valuable discussion time talking about something you did not mean.

Listen not only to what is said but to who is saying it. If you have to do a bit of selling later, it may help to know who resists your idea and why.

3. *Accept.* You don't have to agree with whatever criticism is leveled at your idea, but you'd better accept that the people leveling it take their criticism seriously. You want to be careful not to make statements that appear to be put-downs or ridicule. Avoid, for example, such statements as "How in the world did you come to that conclusion?" or "Come on; you're really reaching." Sometimes you might even blurt out, "That's ridiculous." Then the fight might be on.

Even if you don't say things that distress others, you may show disapproval in your face. Some people can listen quietly to others, yet have an expression on their face that is easily interpreted as "What nonsense." That kind of nonverbal communicating hardly makes friends and influences people—in your favor, at any rate.

4. *Make it a group issue.* If you hang back from defending your idea, you may be pleasantly surprised to hear someone else take up the defense instead. That person probably has more credibility and influence than you in this situation because

(Text continues on page 71.)

MANAGING CONFLICT AS THE TEAM LEADER

There will be times when a conflict between two members of the team prevents each member from being fully effective—and keeps the team from moving forward. Try to resolve the conflict quickly by asking each party to the dispute to respond to the following statements in private. Ask them to use only positive statements—nothing "finger pointing" such as "He should stop doing. . . ." Then bring the two together and help them look for ways to boil their responses down to objectives that both of them can agree with. Finally, show what has to be done to satisfy those objectives, who does what, and when.

- I believe that he (she) should:

  _____

  _____

  _____

- He (she) believes that I should:

  _____

  _____

  _____

- I believe that I should:

  _____

  _____

  _____

- He (she) believes that he (she) should:

  _____

  _____

  _____

he or she is nonpartisan. But if no one else responds immediately, just sit quietly. You don't always have to speak up just because other members want to address you on the idea, unless they ask you questions that only you can answer.

If one or two people address their comments to you, and the discussion seems too narrowly focused, you can make the discussion a group issue by saying, "I've heard extensively how Jane and Howard feel about my idea, but I'd find it valuable to hear how others look at it." That's often all it takes for others to join in, and you may wind up with a lively and broad discussion. You can then relax again.

5. *Answer.* If the group discussion still leaves something missing or to be desired, you may want to respond to some of the disagreement. When you do, address the group, not your critic. Remember, you've made it a group issue now. Don't take it back.

IV

CREATIVITY AND EFFECTIVENESS IN TEAM MEETINGS

CHAPTER 11

GROUP PROBLEM SOLVING AND DECISION MAKING

The chief advantage of using your team to solve problems and make decisions is that you bring different resources together to interact and to develop more options than you would be able to enjoy if each member were acting on his or her own. There is no question that the synergy in an effective team produces more than the sum of its parts.

There are a number of ways to enhance the creativity of the team problem-solving process—and to arrive at consensus decisions:

1. *Keep the group small.* You want to encourage full participation, which is more likely to occur in a limited time with a small group than with a large group. Some experts say that a group with between five and nine members is most effective.

2. *Announce the meeting in advance.* Define the issue to be discussed, and invite participants to come prepared with ideas and possible solutions. Groups usually are better at evaluating ideas than generating them. Individuals are better at coming up with ideas.

3. *Use a round robin to collect people's ideas.* Go around the room and ask people, one by one, to mention the ideas or solutions they've developed. List them on a flip chart or a blackboard. During the round robin, there is to be no criticism or evaluation. The only questions permitted are those that seek clarification of a listed item.

4. *Encourage people to discuss the idea with the group, not with the originator.* Once it is on the table, the idea is a group issue, to be dealt with by the group. Questions and comments

persistently addressed to the member who submitted the idea can make him or her feel ganged up on. The other members shouldn't put pressure on the person to defend or argue for the idea.

5. *Rephrase criticism in a positive way.* A frequent negative comment is "We tried that, and it didn't work." A helpful response could be "What's in this version that wasn't in the one that didn't fly?" Or "How have conditions changed to encourage us to retry the idea?"

6. *Ask for positive remarks from negative people.* When negative comments proliferate, create two columns, "pro" and "con," on a flip chart. Then ask each person who has made negative comments to put his or her objection in the "con" column, and then something for the "pro" side. This approach reduces defensiveness, broadens thinking, and encourages people to look for solutions rather than problems.

7. *Set an example by not defending your ideas.* When your idea is criticized, you may feel a protective instinct. Let others carry the ball. Remind the team that your idea is a group issue. If they misunderstand what you've proposed, clarify it, but don't defend. Others will catch on and emulate your behavior.

ARRIVING AT A CONSENSUS DECISION

Consensus decisions take time and patience, but the decisions that result from a consensus are usually superior to decisions made by the brightest member of the group. This is probably because a group can generate and more realistically evaluate a greater number of options. There is usually a deeper commitment on the part of team members to carrying out the decisions, since the members have been heard, their contributions have been fully considered, and they have left the conference table believing that the product of their discussions is the very best it could have been. When there is a consensus, people don't just go along with the decision. Rather, they invest themselves in it.

Aside from allowing enough time to make a good decision, and having the patience to work through as many options as can be generated by team members, you can take four steps that contribute greatly to a consensus decision:

1. *Encourage all participants to have a full say.* Create an atmosphere in which all team members feel free to voice even their slightest concerns and reservations. Make sure that no one gets put down or shut out. In the first stages of the discussion, you may want to discourage debate so everyone can have his or her say. Accept the fact that people are genuinely concerned about what they express, and respect contributions even though you don't agree with them or regard them as major. People will soon express freely what is on their minds if they know they will not be belittled or besieged.

2. *Emphasize positives.* Participants sometimes find it easier to talk about what they dislike about a proposal than what they think will work. From time to time, sum up what the people in the discussion think is good or might work. "We seem to have a problem with the initial cash outlay, but we're all agreed that the results should turn positive in less than ninety days." Or "It's a complex program, but everyone seems to feel that we have the necessary personnel and expertise to handle it, if we want to go ahead with it."

3. *Find out how serious the negatives are.* Sarah has been throwing up all sorts of objections to the plan that Tracy has submitted. You listen carefully to what appears to be an unbroken stream of flaws. Suddenly it occurs to you that most of the flaws have to do with the schedule for implementing the plan. Sarah thinks it's far too tight and will cause problems for other people, many of which she has described. So you intervene: "Sarah, suppose we were to introduce this in three stages instead of two, and over six months instead of four. Do you think that might solve some of your fears about the plan?" She thinks it over for a long moment, then answers, "Well, it would certainly increase the chances for acceptance."

Until you critically examine what Sarah is saying, it looks as if her resistance is too formidable. But it turns out that her negative feelings are not as pervasive and as serious as you thought at first.

Sometimes people value the chance to express their reservations even when they don't regard them as insuperable barriers. They may also believe, in the spirit of consensus, that they have an obligation to bring up any possible negative, no matter how minor. When they find that others don't share their fears, they let go of them. Once people start thinking in a positive manner, they often come up with suggestions on their own about how the problems can be solved.

4. *Keep summing up the areas of agreement.* With sufficient discussion and a clear respect within the group for everyone's contributions, you can expect the areas of agreement to widen. Emphasize the movement that the group is making toward unanimity by periodically summarizing the areas on which everyone agrees. Eventually you come to a point where problems and disagreements seem to melt away. People begin to realize that they are approaching a decision that is acceptable to all—that the group is working together to remove all obstacles. Consensus may then emerge quite suddenly.

CHAPTER 12

HOLDING EFFECTIVE MEETINGS

Since teams accomplish much of their work in meetings, it is important that the meetings run as effectively and efficiently as possible. An effective meeting starts on time, because people value the time of other team members. It is timed to ensure optimum concentration by members—a maximum of ninety minutes is about right. A meeting should begin with a clear statement of the problem, issue, or objective, and discussion begins only when it is clear that every participant understands the meeting's purpose and what it is to accomplish. When possible, information that will help members generate solutions and conclusions is distributed before the meeting begins. The chair or appointed leader performs formal leadership functions but is ready and willing to share leadership with others as the need arises. He or she is really first among equals.

Team members frequently check with others to make sure they have heard correctly and understand the point of view offered before responding. They feel comfortable offering their ideas and opinions, knowing that other members will support and encourage them even if they do not agree. If one or more members try to exercise control by, for instance, dominating the discussion, judging the relevance of the discussion, or talking excessively, it is the responsibility of the rest of the team to confront and defuse the effort.

Decisions are made by consensus. But before a decision is finally agreed upon, the team tests the possible consequences of the decision on the people affected, the operation, and the decisions being made in other areas of the organization.

When a member makes a contribution to the deliberation, it becomes a group issue and is dealt with by the entire group.

Members never feel isolated or attacked as people. There is a high degree of acceptance of everyone in the group. Expressions of emotions, even anger, are acceptable to the group so long as there is no personal abuse.

Conflicts between members also are treated as issues that involve the team as a whole so that other members feel justified in helping the disputants work through their problems with each other. The group agrees on a solution or a decision only when it is clear that all members have made the contribution they wanted to make. An effective meeting ends at the prescribed time, unless the entire group wishes to extend its discussion. If the objective has not been reached, the group reschedules in order to get a fresh start.

Any decision that the group reaches is tentative until a check is made to ensure that all members of the group are in full accord and committed to it.

All members are committed to the belief that they should discuss group issues in the group and not in extragroup sessions. Those who have second thoughts, questions, or doubts that arise after the adjournment are encouraged to voice them with the rest of the group. They are not squelched.

In an effective meeting, both formal and informal leadership roles are necessary. The formal or appointed leader's role mainly entails setting schedules and communicating with members before the sessions. Most leadership functions can also be undertaken by other team members—and this should be encouraged. Leadership "passed around the table" can tap the various resources that individual members bring to the subject at hand.

The meeting diagnosticator that follows will help you determine not only how effective your meetings are but how effective your leadership has been.

First, add up the number of even-numbered statements you checked. Your maximum count is 15. Next, subtract from your total the sum of odd-numbered statements you checked. To illustrate: If you indicated agreement with 9 even-numbered and 5 odd-numbered statements, your net total is 4.

It is most important that a meeting should reach a unanimous conclusion; it should leave no one frustrated or dissatisfied, for this weakens . . . unity and solidarity.

**—CHIE NAKANE
JAPANESE
WRITER**

(Text continues on page 83.)

DIAGNOSING YOUR MEETINGS

Following are symptoms of both effective and ineffective meetings. For each statement that characterizes the meetings you attend, check the box at the right. If the statement does not apply on a usual basis, leave the box blank.

1. People tend to resist the idea of another meeting. ☐

2. Meetings generally start on time and end on time. ☐

3. When a member contributes an idea or opinion, other members respond to him or her, one to one. ☐

4. Discussions do not begin until it is clear that everyone in the room understands the issue to be decided or the objective to be reached. ☐

5. One or two members slow the meeting down with long, rambling speeches. ☐

6. Our meetings do not end until it is clear that everyone who wants to say something has been able to. ☐

7. People do not address one another but talk about others as if they were not in the room. ☐

8. If the objective of the meeting has not been reached by the time limit, we schedule a follow-up meeting rather than extend the discussion and run overtime. ☐

9. Many ideas and suggestions have to be repeated two or three times before they get a response. ☐

10. The formal leader or chair, in offering his or her position, has no more weight or power than any other member. ☐

11. Sometimes one has to shout to get the attention of others. ☐

12. Often, when people disagree with an idea or comment, they check with the initiator to make sure they've understood before presenting reasons why they disagree. ☐

13. Following many meetings, there are postmortems in people's offices about what went on. ☐

14. Our meetings end with a check to make sure that everyone is committed to the result or goal reached. ☐

15. It's hard to initiate an idea or proposal because there always seems to be someone who puts it down or pokes fun at it. ☐

16. Our problem is not that people decline to participate but that everyone seems to want to talk at once. ☐

(continues)

Diagnosing Your Meetings (continued)

17. After we break up, there is sometimes confusion about what has been resolved or who is responsible for the implementation. ☐

18. Our decisions are always by consensus, with everyone agreeing that they are the best we can make under the circumstances. ☐

19. Meetings often have to be rescheduled when it turns out that the original decisions were based on incomplete information, or when some of the members say they have second thoughts. ☐

20. When one member complains that the meeting has drifted off the track, other members are polled to see whether they agree. ☐

21. Sometimes we agree on one solution or course of action chiefly because the meeting has exhausted everyone. ☐

22. People often say they leave our meetings on an energy high. ☐

23. We seem to spend a disproportionate amount of time at the beginning of most meetings trying to define the problem we're supposed to be working on. ☐

24. While no one likes to see his or her idea criticized, there is a lack of defensiveness and rancor in our meetings when there is disagreement. ☐

25. During our meetings, people arrive late, ask to be excused early, are frequently called out to answer the telephone, and so on. ☐

26. Before most problem-solving or decision-making sessions, we have time to think through the issues so that we come to the conference room prepared. ☐

27. Arguments break out that often seem to have no direct bearing on the issue before the group. ☐

28. When serious conflicts occur between participants, others in the group step in to help them work it out. ☐

29. Getting emotional or showing feelings is strongly discouraged. ☐

30. No one feels attacked or on a "hot seat" when others disagree with him or her, because once the idea is out on the table, members consider it a group issue and it is discussed as such, with everyone talking with everyone else. ☐

Total even numbers   _____

Total odd numbers   _____

If your net total is between 10 and 15, inclusively, you already know that you're experiencing, on the whole, some very constructive and productive meetings. The following analysis of the diagnosticator can point you toward improvement in those areas in which your group is weak or failing to achieve desired effectiveness.

If your net total is between 5 and 9, inclusively, your experience in your meetings is about average, and your frustrations would be immediately identifiable by most people.

Obviously, if your net falls below 5, your meetings breed much resentment for the time they take and the relatively few worthy consequences. The diagnosticator reveals why those meetings constitute a severe impediment to building a team.

Following is an analysis of the statements in the diagnosticator and what they represent, both good and bad.

ANALYZING YOUR DIAGNOSIS

When team members groan at the thought of another meeting, arrive late, leave early, or interrupt the meeting to attend to other business, they are conveying the message that they consider the meetings relatively unimportant or even a waste of time.

In a group that is still fragmented, each member may find that, having voiced a suggestion or a comment, he or she stands alone. Others may zero in, responding on a one-to-one basis, with other members hanging back and providing little or no support, moral or substantive. A related problem is that of people speaking of a member in the third person, as if he or she weren't there. There's little or no feeling of inclusiveness. And when people put down or joke about others' contributions and get away with it, some members will simply refuse to put themselves on the line again. They remain silent or utter completely safe statements that add little to the discussion.

If ideas have to be repeated because they receive no response, or if people have to shout to get attention, the atmosphere can best be described as highly competitive. No one really wants to listen to anyone else. Members are highly self-absorbed.

In many meetings, there is rampant confusion about why people have been called together. The issue that is to be discussed doesn't emerge easily, and people spend a lot of time trying to define the purpose of the conference. No wonder that some decisions are made out of exhaustion. No one wants to spend another minute in the room. There is insufficient effort to get all of the options out on the table, or to test the consequences of each decision. Add the lack of preparation by the people in the meeting, and you'll find many opportunities for poor decision making. It's no surprise that further meetings have to be convened to undo the damage or repair a faulty decision. Since many decisions are decided by majority vote, you'll encounter postmortems in which people stand around, dissect what went on, and express their disagreements and frustrations. And there may also be confusion about what was really decided, who is supposed to do what, and when.

People tend to bring their personal and hidden agendas into meetings, so what they do in the group may be rooted in the biases and perceptions they hold outside the room. Other members are not willing to take a leadership position to help the group achieve its goals. This reluctance to lead manifests itself when some members are allowed to take control with their rambling, disorganized speeches. If they're talking, no one else can—and no one cares enough to place the group's work over the self-indulgence of one or two members.

Finally, in a group in which people can expect no support or sensitivity to the group's well-being, it is hardly surprising that a show of emotion would be threatening. When a member shows deep feeling, he or she could be pulling the mask off others' pretense that everything is harmonious.

EVALUATING YOUR MEETINGS

You'll recall that feedback is essential in motivating people to improve effectiveness. In addition to feedback, people also need

(Text continues on page 86.)

MEETING EVALUATOR

1. How effective was the meeting?

   Explanation: Did people commit themselves to work for what they perceived to be the best interests and most realistic objectives of the group? Were the resources of the group efficiently applied to achieve those objectives? Do you believe that the group's achievement was the best that could have been hoped for?

10 9 8	7 6 5 4	3 2 1
Most effective	Somewhat effective	Ineffective

2. How clear were the group's goals in this meeting?

10 9 8	7 6 5 4	3 2 1
Quite clear	Somewhat clear	Unclear

3. To what extent did the group stay on track in working toward its objectives and avoiding distractions?

10 9 8	7 6 5 4	3 2 1
Completely on track	More on than off	Sidetracked

4. How would you judge your effectiveness in promoting the group's work?

10 9 8	7 6 5 4	3 2 1
Very effective	Somewhat effective	Ineffective

5. To what extent did the group consider your contributions?

10 9 8	7 6 5 4	3 2 1
Totally	Somewhat	Not at all

   (continues)

Meeting Evaluator (continued)

6. How free did you feel to express your opinions and to make contributions in the group?

   10   9   8   7   6   5   4   3   2   1
      Totally   Somewhat   Not at all

7. Overall, what was your level of satisfaction with the meeting?

   10   9   8   7   6   5   4   3   2   1
   Well-satisfied   Somewhat satisfied   Dissatisfied

guidelines to better performance. As your team develops, members want to be able to see not only their individual progress in effectiveness but also how the group is pulling together.

A very easy and graphic way to chart people's perceptions of their own effectiveness and that of the group is to evaluate each meeting immediately after it is adjourned. Initially, you may wish to keep the evaluations anonymous. Simply have each member fill out the following form and pass it around to you. You can record the ratings on a blackboard or flip chart and average them.

In time, as people grow in openness and comfort, it will not matter so much whether they sign their names or not. Signing the form could even be helpful in a case in which one person registers much lower ratings for a meeting than other members. The group may wish to examine the reasons for the member's dissatisfaction with the meeting and with the group. It's possible that the unhappy member sensed certain impediments to his or her effectiveness that other members didn't discern—but need to know about.

CHARTING THE PROGRESS OF YOUR MEETINGS

Using the individual evaluation forms, you can arrive at an average rating for each category and each meeting. But since your aim is to build a team, you may wish to keep track of your progress toward more effectiveness, more support, more openness, and greater overall satisfaction. Following is a ratings chart to use over an extensive period of time—say ten meetings. The average evaluation for each meeting, derived from the individual forms, is posted using the numbers on the vertical axis. On the horizontal axis are the numbers of the sessions evaluated.

You may maintain a master chart for each of the seven questions

MASTER EVALUATION CHART

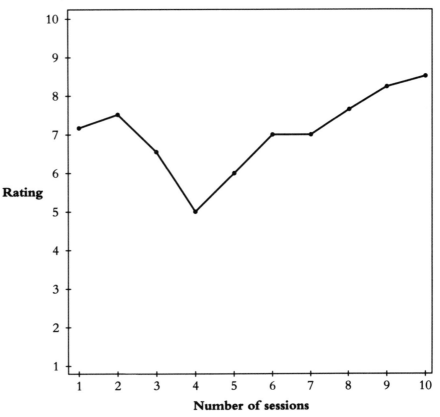

on the individual evaluation form, or you may select a different color of pen or marker for each of the seven questions you want to chart progress in.

Incidentally, don't be surprised if, as you begin to chart your progress in holding meetings, the ratings begin high and then take a dip before climbing again. Initially, people tend to be very cautious in their assessments of themselves and the group. It takes a certain amount of risk taking to be able to say publicly, "I don't think we were very effective today." As the group members begin to take the evaluations seriously and develop confidence that they won't be punished for assessing the meetings honestly, the rating line will dip and then rise again. And as it rises, it constitutes a powerful reinforcer for the effective behavior that people demonstrate in the meetings.

PART

EVALUATING AND REWARDING TEAM PROGRESS

CHAPTER 13

TEAM PERFORMANCE EVALUATION

There are at least four ways that a team can be evaluated on its performance:

1. Individual members by their permanent managers, if the members are part of a temporary group (such as a committee or task force) or a part-time group (such as a quality circle)
2. Individual members by the team leader
3. The whole team through evaluations such as those shown in Chapter 12, which track the progress of the team in its meetings
4. Individual members by their peers on the team

Regardless of who does the evaluating, team members should receive evaluations based on their contributions to the team's success, as well as on their own performance outside the team if their membership is not full-time.

In this chapter you'll find a peer evaluation form that can also serve as a guide for the team leader to evaluate each member. There is one important caveat to the form: The categories really measure inputs, not outputs. Thus, the evaluation for each member has to be measured against the progress of the group toward its stated and agreed-upon goals. Performance evaluations that are based totally on activity broadcast a self-defeating message: that results are not important.

(Text continues on page 94.)

PEER FEEDBACK EVALUATION

In each category, circle the number that you believe best represents the usual behavior of [*name of team member*]:

- Initiates ideas.

10 9 8	7 6 5 4	3 2 1
Frequently offers ideas and solutions.	Initiates only moderately, but supports initiating by others.	Tends to let others take most of the initiative and often reserves support.

- Facilitates the introduction of new ideas.

10 9 8	7 6 5 4	3 2 1
Actively encourages others to contribute without worrying about agreement.	Provides support for ideas with which he or she agrees.	Often resists the introduction of new ideas; looks for flaws.

- Is directed toward group goals.

10 9 8	7 6 5 4	3 2 1
Often helps to identify and clarify goals for the group.	Sometimes helps the group define its goals; sometimes confuses it with side issues.	Tends to place priority on own goals at the expense of group's.

- Manages conflict.

10 9 8	7 6 5 4	3 2 1
Regards conflict as helpful in promoting different perspectives and in sharpening the differences in views.	Generally disengages from conflict.	Tries to smooth over points of disagreement; plays a pacifying role.

- Demonstrates support for others.

10 9 8	7 6 5 4	3 2 1
Actively encourages the participation of others and asserts their right to be heard.	Encourages certain members part of the time, but does not encourage all members.	Does not offer support or encouragement for other members.

- Reveals feelings.

10 9 8	7 6 5 4	3 2 1
Openly expresses feelings about issues; ensures that feelings parallel views.	Sometimes disguises feelings or tries to keep them to self.	Denies both the existence of own feelings and the importance of expressing them in the group.

- Displays openness.

10 9 8	7 6 5 4	3 2 1
Freely and clearly expresses self on issues so that others know where he or she stands.	Sometimes employs tact and speaks circumspectly to camouflage real views.	Is vague about views on issues, even contradictory when pressed.

- Confronts issues and behavior.

10 9 8	7 6 5 4	3 2 1
Freely expresses views on difficult issues and on team members' nonproductive behavior.	Is cautious about taking a visible position on issues and on others' actions without first ensuring widespread approval.	Actively avoids issues and any conflict by talking about "safe" issues that are irrelevant to current group work.

(continues)

Peer Feedback Evaluation (continued)

- Shares leadership.

10 9 8	7 6 5 4	3 2 1
Assumes responsibility for guiding the group when own resources are needed or when problems lend themselves to his or her solving.	Competes with other members for visibility and influence.	Dominates group discussions and exerts disproportionate influence that subverts group progress.

- Exhibits proper demeanor in decision-making process.

10 9 8	7 6 5 4	3 2 1
Actively seeks a full exploration of all feasible options.	Becomes impatient with a deliberate pace in generating and evaluating all options when he or she does not concur with them.	Moves strongly toward early closure of discussion to vote on a preferred option.

PEER FEEDBACK

In a well-developed team that is characterized by openness and supportiveness, members know that they can benefit from their peers' feedback. The more each member knows about the impact of his or her behavior on other members of the team, the better advised the member is in adjusting that behavior to be even more effective. It may be a matter of sharpening the member's demonstrated competence in a group or of eliminating some practices that others find unhelpful and unattractive.

Peer evaluations are best held quarterly. Each team member completes an evaluation form for all other members. Then members can meet in one-on-one sessions or as a group to discuss the evaluations. The advantage of the group setting is that all members are present to hear feedback and are free to ask the evaluator why he or she has selected a particular rating. Ratings among peers will vary, of course. But, for instance, if Charles' rating of Norma is very disparate from what Norma's other peers give her, it should become a group issue: The relationship between Charles and Norma, as evidenced in his evaluation, may need some working on and talking about. Other team members can be supportive of both as Charles and Norma work on the relationship.

The downside of group peer feedback is that a member who receives several unfavorable evaluations may feel threatened. However, the group can provide support to help him or her overcome the negative reactions to the ratings. The message can be "You're okay as a person, but we believe you can be more effective as a member of the team. We want you to be, and we're willing to help you." That message can be a powerful incentive for anyone to find ways to be a more valuable team member.

Please read the group peer feedback evaluation form with explanations for the various ratings, on pages 93 and 94.

CHAPTER 14

REWARDING SUCCESSFUL TEAM PERFORMANCE

Be certain to reward successful performance. Good intentions, activity, hustle and bustle, loyalty, and goodwill may be valuable, but they constitute inputs. Outputs count. When team members have accomplished what you have asked them to, reward them. That doesn't mean you can't set subgoals on the road to the final goals and reward the team's progress as it reaches each subgoal. But achieving the final goal is what counts.

Rewarding Successful Performance

1. *Reward soon after the accomplishment.* Don't wait. When people have done well and are feeling good about what they've done, reinforcing their success with a valued reward has great impact on future actions.

2. *Be specific about what you're rewarding.* Let them know what accomplishments you're rewarding them for. General compliments such as "Great job!" don't convey useful information. What made it great?

3. *Be consistent.* When you get the results you asked for, recognize the team's success. Never take for granted that team members know how great your appreciation is.

> **Rewards should go to teams as a whole.**
>
> —TOM PETERS
> BUSINESS
>   WRITER AND
>   CONSULTANT

How you reward team members depends in part on what you are rewarding and why. Your rewards should focus team members' attention on the importance of both building and maintaining team success. The following list presents you with a range of possibilities.

EMPLOYEE REWARDS OF EFFECTIVE TEAMWORK

☐ More responsible tasks
☐ More freedom over their goals
☐ Praise from you to them
☐ Praise to higher management
☐ Training to increase their competence
☐ More control by them over how they work
☐ More opportunities to act as an advisory group for you
☐ More control over scheduling of members
☐ Publicity throughout the organization
☐ Salary increases
☐ Days off
☐ Lunch or dinner on you or the organization
☐ Certificates or plaques
☐ New or better furnishings
☐ More advanced equipment
☐ Plants or books
☐ Party
☐ Coaching for career opportunities
☐ Freedom to select tasks and projects
☐ "Thank you"

NOTES

NOTES

NOTES

NOTES

NOTES

NOTES